THE TERMINATOR™

2029-1984

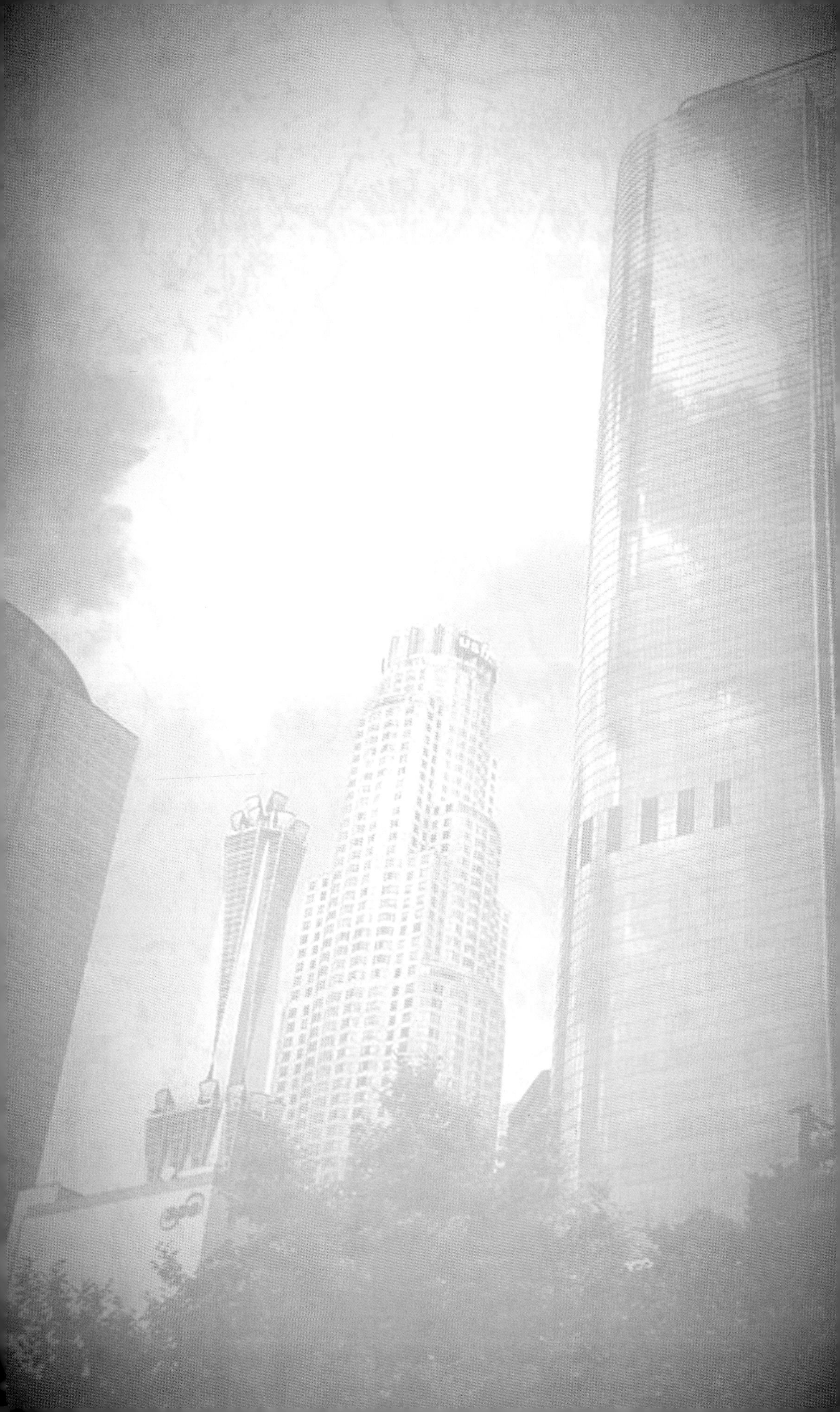

THE TERMINATOR™

2029-1984

SCRIPT
ZACK WHEDON

ART
ANDY MACDONALD

LETTERING
NATE PIEKOS OF BLAMBOT®

COLORS
DAN JACKSON

COVER ART
MASSIMO CARNEVALE

DARK HORSE BOOKS®

PRESIDENT AND PUBLISHER
MIKE RICHARDSON

EDITOR
SIERRA HAHN

ASSISTANT EDITOR
BRENDAN WRIGHT

DESIGNER
STEPHEN REICHERT

STUDIO CANAL

THE TERMINATOR™: 2029–1984

This volume collects issues #1 through #3 of *The Terminator: 2029* and issues #1 through #3 of *The Terminator: 1984* from Dark Horse Comics.

Published by Dark Horse Books
A division of Dark Horse Comics, Inc.
10956 SE Main Street
Milwaukie, OR 97222

DarkHorse.com

To find a comics shop in your area, call the Comic Shop Locator Service toll-free at (888) 266-4226.

Library of Congress Cataloging-in-Publication Data

Whedon, Zack.
The terminator, 2029-1984 / script, Zack Whedon ; art, Andy MacDonald ; colors, Dan Jackson ; lettering, Nate Piekos ; cover art, Massimo Carnevale. -- 1st ed.
p. cm.
"Collects The Terminator: 2029 #1-#3 and The Terminator: 1984 #1-#3."
ISBN 978-1-59582-647-3
1. Graphic novels. I. MacDonald, Andy, artist. II. Title.
PN6727.W447T47 2011
741.5'973--dc22

2010048981

First edition: June 2011

1 3 5 7 9 10 8 6 4 2

Printed at Midas Printing International, Ltd., Huizhou, China

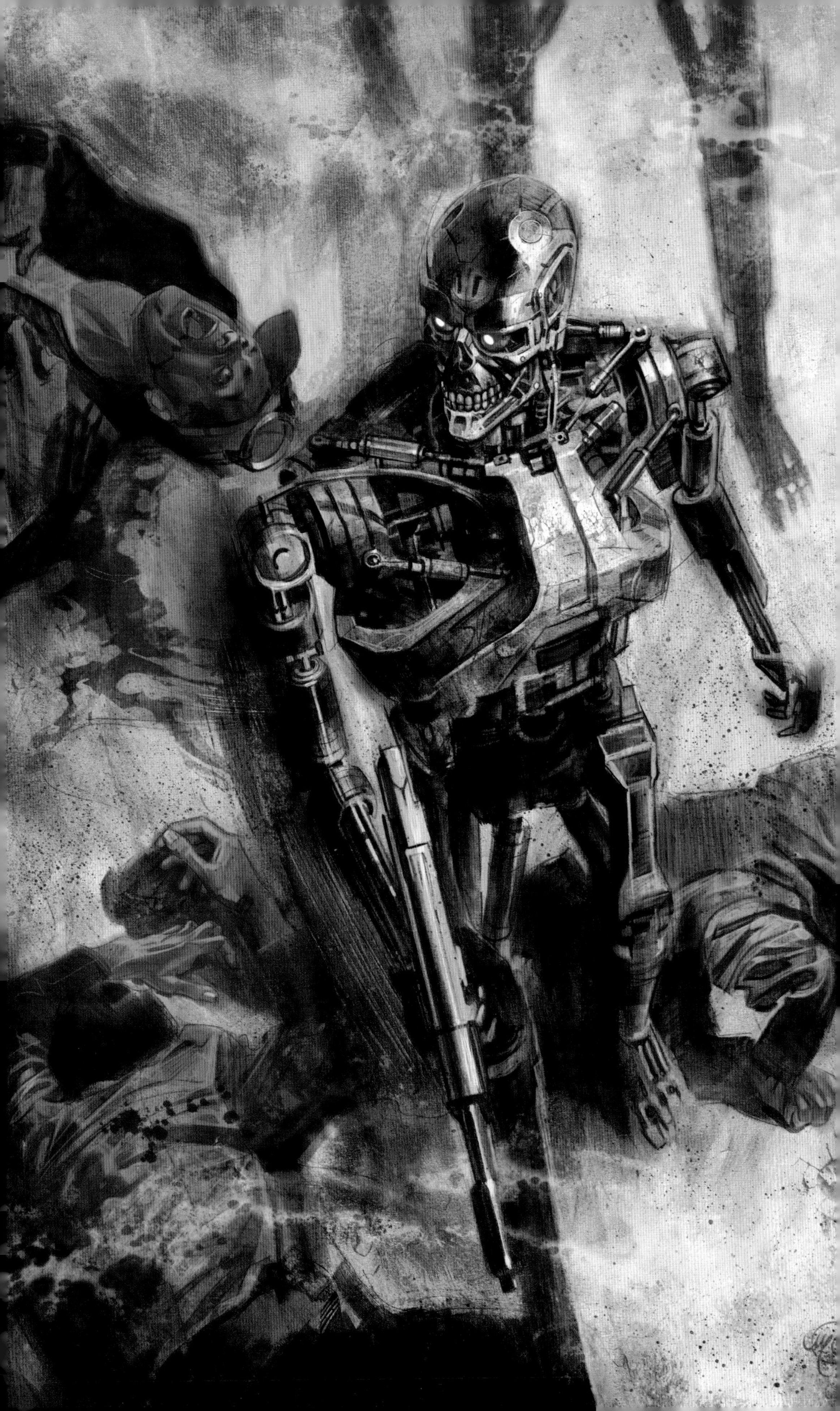

2029

It's been several decades since the computer system Skynet became self-aware and launched a nuclear strike against humanity. Ever since, humans have been at war with Skynet and its army of Hunter-Killer drones and deadly Terminator cyborgs. The human resistance is led by John Connor, trained from childhood to fight the machines by his mother, Sarah Connor, who knew the war was imminent. With Connor's Resistance gaining ground, Skynet developed a mysterious new model of Terminator and is experimenting with time travel to crush the Resistance before it can begin.

Amidst the fighting small colonies of human survivors are trying to persevere in this hostile landscape—with Kyle Reese and his band of friends leading the charge.

PASADENA, CA - 2029 A.D.
I LOVE YOU, PAIGE.
THAT'S NICE.
KISS ME?
NOPE.
ALL RIGHT... BUT IT'S YOUR LOSS. I'M ONE OF THE GREAT, UNDISCOVERED SEXUAL TALENTS.
UNDISCOVERED IS RIGHT.
Whoa, I MAKE FUN OF MYSELF SO THAT YOU WILL NOT. YOU CAN'T JUST PILE ON LIKE THAT.
YOU'RE DISTRACTING ME, BEN.
SORRY... THIS POST IS BORING.
BORING IS GOOD. **BORING** MEANS WE'RE NOT BEING SHOT AT.
FOR A CHANGE.

SORRY ABOUT THE "UNDISCOVERED" THING.
THAT'S COOL.
NICE SUNSET.
YEAH. CLEAR SKIES.
dink
AHH!
WHAT THE HELL?!

HAHA!
RICO, YOU PRICK!
SHIFT'S OVER, LOVEBIRDS! I'M ON MY WAY UP!
LOVEBIRDS?
IS IT SO CRAZY?
SHUT UP.
MAN, I WALKED RIGHT UP ON YOU GUYS!
IF I WERE A SIX HUNDRED, YOU GUYS WOULD BE TOAST!
IF YOU WERE A SIX HUNDRED, YOU'D BE WAY MORE CHARMING.
AHHHH!
CRAK
DON'T THROW ROCKS AT BEN.

YOUR HEAD ALL RIGHT?
YEAH.
DO YOU HEAR THAT?
Huh?
RMMM
WHAT IS THAT? H-K?
SOUNDS LIKE SOMETHING ELSE...
VROOM

SKREEEECH
HEY, KIDS.
KYLE!
YOU'RE BACK!
WHEN DID YOU GET HOME?
JUST NOW.
HOP IN. I'LL GIVE YOU A RIDE BACK TO CAMP.

WE WERE BEGINNING TO THINK...YOU KNOW.
HAD SOME CLOSE CALLS, THAT'S FOR SURE.
BUT YOU DIDN'T FIND ANYONE?
NO.
I SCOUTED PRETTY FAR TOO. ONLY FOLKS I CROSSED WANTED TO GO IT ALONE.
THEY THINK THE COLONY'S A MAGNET.
I THINK THE WAY YOU HAVE TO LIVE OUT THERE, ON YOUR OWN, IT'S NOT HUMAN. LIVING LIKE THAT ISN'T WORTH FIGHTING TO PRESERVE.
AMEN.

PASADENA ONE SURVIVOR COLONY POP. 4,672.
HERE WE ARE.
WELCOME HOME.
IT'S NICE TO BE BACK. I ACTUALLY STARTED TO MISS YOU GUYS.
WE MISSED YOU TOO.
KYLE REESE, SERGEANT, TECH-COM DN38416.
HOW MUCH *METAL* WHILE I WAS GONE?
NOTHING.
IT WAS QUIET?
NOT A PEEP.
DON'T KNOW WHAT THAT'S ABOUT.

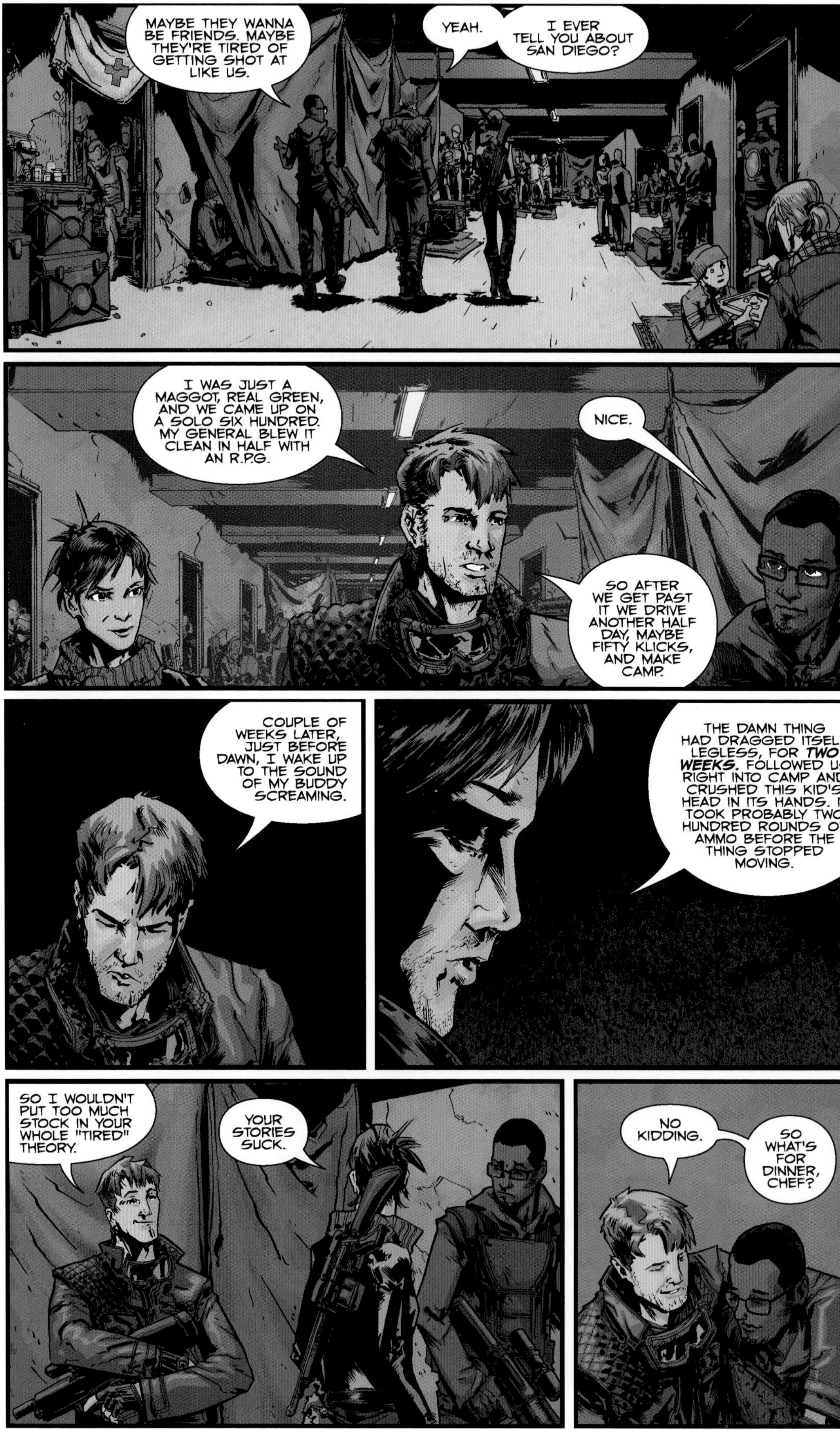
MAYBE THEY WANNA BE FRIENDS. MAYBE THEY'RE TIRED OF GETTING SHOT AT LIKE US.
YEAH.
I EVER TELL YOU ABOUT SAN DIEGO?
I WAS JUST A MAGGOT, REAL GREEN, AND WE CAME UP ON A SOLO SIX HUNDRED. MY GENERAL BLEW IT CLEAN IN HALF WITH AN R.P.G.
NICE.
SO AFTER WE GET PAST IT WE DRIVE ANOTHER HALF DAY, MAYBE FIFTY KLICKS, AND MAKE CAMP.
COUPLE OF WEEKS LATER, JUST BEFORE DAWN, I WAKE UP TO THE SOUND OF MY BUDDY SCREAMING.
THE DAMN THING HAD DRAGGED ITSELF, LEGLESS, FOR *TWO WEEKS.* FOLLOWED US RIGHT INTO CAMP AND CRUSHED THIS KID'S HEAD IN ITS HANDS. IT TOOK PROBABLY TWO HUNDRED ROUNDS OF AMMO BEFORE THE THING STOPPED MOVING.
SO I WOULDN'T PUT TOO MUCH STOCK IN YOUR WHOLE "TIRED" THEORY.
YOUR STORIES SUCK.
NO KIDDING.
SO WHAT'S FOR DINNER, CHEF?

IF I NEVER EAT ANOTHER CANNED PEAR, IT'LL BE TOO DAMNED SOON.
SCRAAAAPE
DON'T TELL BEN. HE JUST WENT TO GET MORE, AND YOU KNOW HOW SENSITIVE HE IS ABOUT HIS "COOKING."
HE AMAZES ME.
I'VE SEEN SOME UGLY STUFF-- HELL, WE ALL HAVE... BUT IT DOESN'T HOLD A CANDLE TO WHAT THAT KID'S BEEN THROUGH.
AND STILL EVERY WORD OUT OF HIS MOUTH MAKES ME LAUGH.
SO WHAT'S THE STORY WITH YOU TWO, huh?
YOU GONNA TIE THE KNOT ANYTIME SOON?
KYLE.
SHUT UP.
C'MON. THE ONLY PERSON IN THIS WHOLE COLONY WHO DOESN'T KNOW YOU TWO ARE IN LOVE IS *YOU.*
YOU GOT A FUNNY WAY OF SHUTTING UP.
I JUST CALL 'EM LIKE I SEE 'EM.
WHAT ARE YOU GUYS TALKING ABOUT?
NOTHIN'. I'M GOING TO BED.
YOU DON'T WANT DESSERT?
THANKS.
WHAT WAS THAT?

WHAT THE...
HEY, NORTHWEST, COME IN. I'M SEEING SOME MOVEMENT, DOESN'T LOOK LIKE METAL THOUGH. YOU GOT ANYONE OUT ON PATROL?
NORTHWEST, DO YOU READ?
NORTHWEST. COME IN.
DO YOU READ, NORTHWEST?
C'MON, MAN.

clink
Huh?
JESUS CHRIST! YOU SCARED THE PISS OUT OF ME!
WHAT'S YOUR NAME AND RANK?!
HEY, MAN, WHAT'S YOUR NAME AND RANK?!

BLAM
BLAM
BLAM
WHAT'RE YOU LOOKIN' AT?
NOTHING.
HEY.
NOBODY.
WHO IS THIS?
OBVIOUSLY IT'S SOMEBODY.
...SARAH CONNOR.

HOW THE HELL DID YOU GET A PICTURE OF SARAH CONNOR?
JOHN GAVE IT TO ME.
JOHN **CONNOR?** ALL-POWERFUL LEADER OF THE RESISTANCE, JOHN CONNOR?
WHEN?
YEARS AGO.
HE GAVE YOU A PICTURE OF HIS **MOM?**
YEAH, HAND IT OVER.
THAT'S THE CREEPIEST THING I'VE EVER HEARD.
"HEY, BUDDY, NICE FIGHTIN'. HERE'S A PICTURE OF MY MOM."
GO TO SLEEP.

THOOM
THOOM
THOOM
THOOM
BOOM
WHAT WAS THAT?
I'M GONNA CHECK IT OUT.
GATHER AS MANY PEOPLE AS YOU CAN AND HEAD TO THE SOUTHEAST TUNNEL. IF THINGS GET HAIRY, YOU KNOW WHAT TO DO.
YEAH.
PAIGE!

BOOM
THE COLONY'S LOST. WE'VE GOT TO GET OUT OF HERE WHILE WE CAN.
DEAR GOD.
REESE! IT'S OVER. LET'S GO!
IT'S OVER!

COME ON. WE'VE GOT TO BE READY TO EVACUATE.
PAIGE, THIS IS MY HOME. I'M NOT GOING ANYWHERE.
BOOM
JESUS. THAT WAS CLOSE.
INSIDE THE PERIMETER FOR SURE.
WE'RE GOING.
NOW.
LET'S GO! EVERYONE OUT!

SCREEECH
LET'S GO, YOU SON OF A BITCH.

CLIK
BOOM

C'MON! EVERYONE IN!
WHAT ABOUT KYLE?
HE'LL BE FINE. WE HAVE TO GO.
BEN. IT'S OKAY. HE'LL BE FINE.
OKAY. BUCKLE UP.

BRBBRRRRR
SMASH

WAKE UP.
BEN. WAKE UP.
IS IT ALREADY MY SHIFT AGAIN?
NO.
WHERE ARE WE? WHY DID WE STOP?
WE BROKE DOWN. NEED YOU TO TAKE A LOOK.
WE'RE SUNK. NO WAY WE CAN GET THIS STARTED AGAIN.
DAMMIT.

THEY WALKED RIGHT IN.
SIX HUNDREDS?
NO. SOMETHING NEW. THEY LOOKED HUMAN. EXACTLY.
I DON'T KNOW HOW YOU DEFEND AGAINST THAT...
I PROMISED PEOPLE THEY'D BE SAFE THERE. THEY TRUSTED ME.
YOU GAVE US A HOME, KYLE, A LIFE. IT'S NOT YOUR FAULT THEY TOOK IT AWAY.
GATHER EVERYONE UP. WE NEED TO START WALKING. EAST. HEAD FOR THE NEAREST COLONY.
IT'S OUR ONLY CHANCE.

HEY, REESE, DID YOU RADIO FOR TRANSPORT?
TRIED. DEAD AIR. ONCE WE HIT THE TREE LINE WE'LL TRY AGAIN. WE'RE TOO EXPOSED RIGHT NOW.
HOW LONG BEFORE SOMEONE GETS HERE, YOU THINK?
COULD BE DAYS. IF WE MANAGE TO REACH SOMEONE AT ALL.

I BURIED MY WHOLE FAMILY THERE, BEN.
I KNOW.
I GUESS IT WAS CRAZY TO THINK WE WOULDN'T GET DEMOLISHED EVENTUALLY.
IT WAS HOME.
CRAZY OR NOT, THAT PLACE SAVED ME. I WAS THERE SIX YEARS.
THE NEXT PLACE WILL BE HOME TOO, PAIGE.
YOU SEE THAT?
YEAH...
MAYBE WE SHOULD--

SONOFA!
EVERYONE DOWN!
AAH!
BAM
THOOM
THOOM

BLAM
BLAM
THEY'RE GONNA WALK RIGHT UP ON US! GET EVERYONE BACK. I'LL LAY DOWN COVER!
EVERYONE MOVE OUT!
RUN!
AHHH!
KRAK

BAM
BLAM
BOOM
KLIK
KLIK
KLIK
WHAT THE...?

RRMMMMMBBLLLL
YEEHAW!

THOOM
THOOM
HURRY UP! GET IN!
C'MON! C'MON!
EVERYONE IN! LET'S GO!

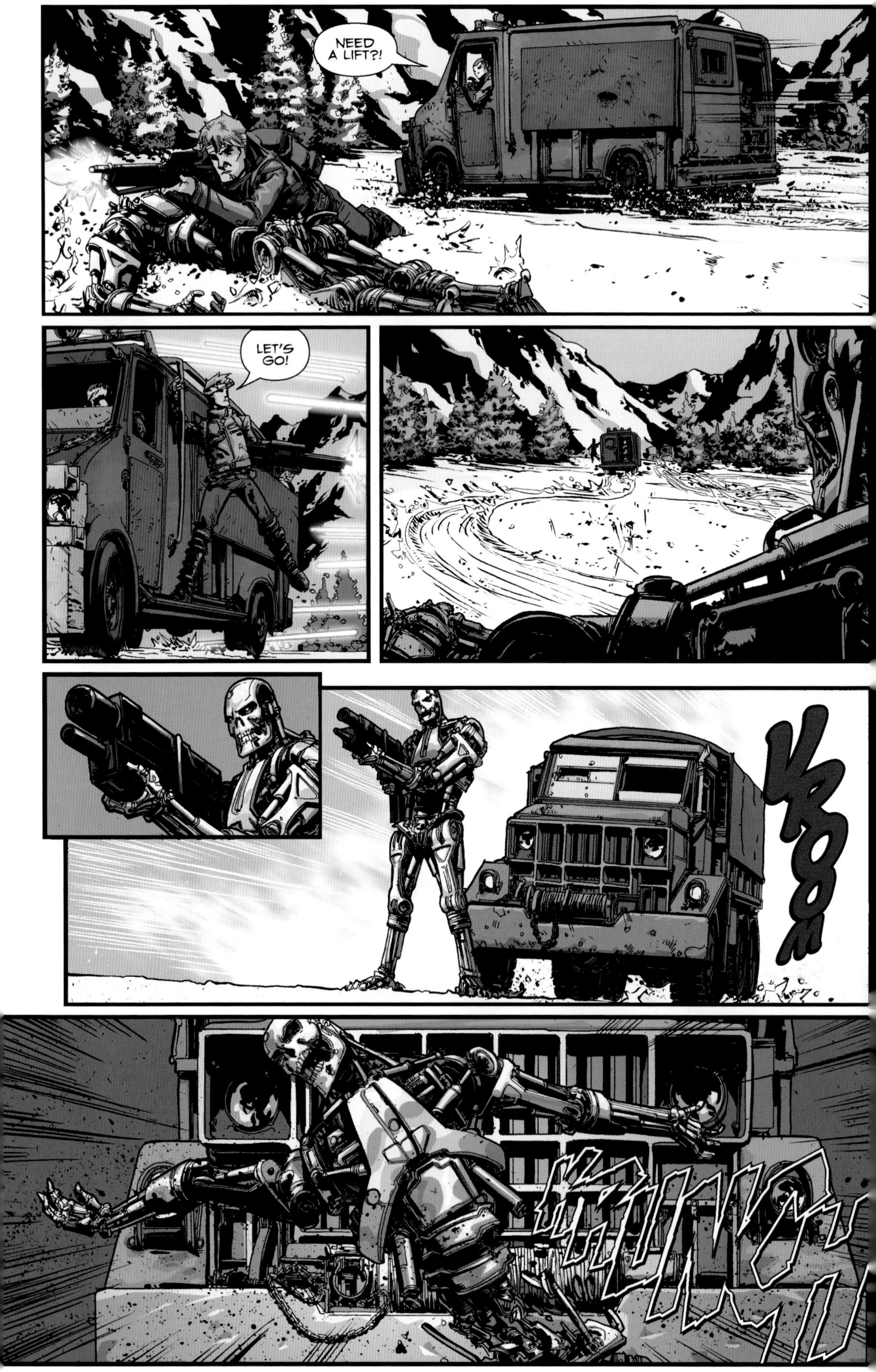
NEED A LIFT?!
LET'S GO!
VROOM

YOU ALL RIGHT?
YEAH.
WHO THE HELL ARE THESE GUYS?
IT'S YANKEE COMPANY. OR WHAT'S LEFT OF 'EM.
YOU KNOW THEM?
JUST HEARD ABOUT 'EM.
THEY'RE RESISTANCE?
THEY WERE. DIDN'T LIKE TAKING ORDERS. JUST LIKED KILLIN'.
THAT DIDN'T GO OVER WELL WITH COMMAND.
NOW THEY'RE ON THEIR OWN.
PAIGE!

THUD
AAH!
CRUNCH

KRSHH
AAHHH!
ZZZZT
OOF!

NO ONE'S GIVING ME A STRAIGHT ANSWER ABOUT WHY WE STOPPED.
NO ONE KNOWS WHO THE HELL YOU ARE.
KYLE REESE, SERGEANT TECH-COM, DN38416.
WHO ARE YOU?
I'M RED.
POMONA'S THE CLOSEST BASE BUT WE'RE NOT HEADING THAT WAY, ARE WE?
NOT JUST YET. MAKING A QUICK DETOUR. WE WEREN'T PLANNING ON PICKING UP A PACK OF STRAYS.
DETOUR WHERE?
FOLLOW ME. I'LL SHOW YA.

OUR SCOUT SPOTTED IT A FEW WEEKS AGO.
WHAT THE HELL IS THAT?
DON'T KNOW.
SO WHY ARE WE GOING THERE?
'CUZ IT'S GOOD HUNTIN'.

YOU TOOK DOWN AN EIGHT HUNDRED WITH A PAIR OF NEEDLE-NOSE PLIERS.
WELL...
IT WAS REALLY BRAVE, BEN.
WHAT CAN I SAY? I'M BRAVE.
STUPID TOO. IT COULD HAVE KILLED US BOTH.
YEAH, BUT WHEN YOU'RE CRAZY BRAVE LIKE ME YOU DON'T THINK ABOUT STUFF LIKE THAT.
IT WAS PRETTY AMAZING.
I CAN'T LOSE YOU, PAIGE. I JUST CAN'T.
LET'S SEE THAT ARM.
YOU **SONOFABITCH!**

ARE YOU CRAZY?!
GET OFFA ME!
Whoa Whoa Whoa!
THESE PEOPLE NEED TO GET TO A BASE! THEY NEED PROTECTION. WE'VE ALREADY LOST TOO MANY.
NOBODY MADE Y'ALL COME WITH US.
FOUR BILLION DEAD AND THEY MANAGE TO MISS THIS ASSHOLE.
NOW WHAT KIND OF ATTITUDE IS THAT?
YOU'RE GOING TO GET YOURSELVES KILLED AND THESE PEOPLE ARE GOING TO BE STRANDED.
YOU KNOW, YOU'RE RIGHT. IT IS DANGEROUS. I'M A LITTLE CONCERNED FOR MY SAFETY.
YOU'RE PUTTING PEOPLE'S LIVES IN JEOPARDY SO YOU CAN GET AN ADRENALINE FIX FIGHTING EIGHT HUNDREDS!
IF ONLY WE HAD A WAR HERO, SOMEONE WITH THE TRAINING AND EXPERTISE TO MAKE SURE WE GOT HOME SAFE.
WHADDYA SAY, REESE? WHY DON'T YA COME WITH?

WHAT'S THE PLAN?
LET ME GUESS. THERE ISN'T ONE.
YOU'RE A **RIOT,** YOU KNOW THAT?
WE COME UP FROM THE SOUTH, TWO MORE FROM THE WEST, AND TWO FROM THE NORTH.
WE PIN 'EM AGAINST THAT BUILDING AND WE'LL HAVE THE BASTARDS ON ALL SIDES.
IT'LL BE A DAMN TURKEY SHOOT.
GENERAL LEE WOULD BE PROUD.
WHO'S GENERAL LEE?
BOOM

THOOM
BLAM
COME ON! THIS THING'S GONNA BLOW!
LET'S GO!
BOOM

YOU WORRIED ABOUT KYLE?
Nah.
HOW CAN YOU SAY THAT?
HE'S KYLE REESE. HE'LL BE FINE.
THIS SHOULD HOLD YOU UNTIL WE REACH A SURGEON.
EVERY TIME SOMEONE LEAVES THE ROOM I ASSUME THEY'RE NOT COMING BACK.
THAT'S CHEERFUL.
IT'S NOT A CHOICE. IT'S JUST HOW I AM.
HOW THEY MADE ME.
WELL I'M NOT GOING ANYWHERE AND NEITHER IS KYLE.
YOU DON'T KNOW THAT. YOU HAVE NO IDEA.
SO WHAT AM I SUPPOSED TO DO?
HONESTLY? KEEP YOUR DISTANCE.
FROM WHO?
FROM ME, FROM EVERYONE. PROTECT YOURSELF.
OTHERWISE YOU'RE JUST SETTING YOURSELF UP.
PAIGE.
TELL ME I'M WRONG!

YOU'RE **WRONG.**
PEOPLE CONNECT, PAIGE. IT JUST HAPPENS.
PASADENA ONE. IT'S A BAD IDEA, RIGHT? EVERYONE LIVING TOGETHER? MAKES IT EASIER ON THE MACHINES.
BUT PEOPLE NEED PEOPLE.
IT'S DANGEROUS, YEAH, AND IT'S SCARY. SO PEOPLE TELL THEMSELVES THEY'LL GO IT ALONE. THEY DEVOTE THEMSELVES TO THEIR SADNESS.
BUT WE CAN'T HELP IT. WE GRAVITATE TOWARD ONE ANOTHER AND NEXT THING YOU KNOW...
NEXT THING YOU KNOW...
EVEN THOUGH YOU SWORE TO YOURSELF YOU'D NEVER LET YOURSELF GET ATTACHED AGAIN...
NEVER GIVE A SOULLESS MACHINE THE OPPORTUNITY TO TAKE SOMEONE AWAY FROM YOU...
NEXT THING YOU KNOW...

WE SHOULD TAKE SOME OF THESE DRIVES. THERE'S GOTTA BE INTEL HERE THE RESISTANCE CAN USE.
I WAS GONNA SUGGEST BLOWIN' IT SKY HIGH.
WE CAN DO THAT TOO.
THERE'S SOMETHING BACK HERE.
CHA-CHUNK
TSSSSSSSS

GAHH!
Oh GOD...
ARE YOU OKAY?
REESE, I RIGGED THE EXPLOSIVES! LET'S GET THE HELL OUTTA HERE!
COME WITH ME IF YOU WANT TO LIVE.

WE THOUGHT YOU WERE TOAST!
SKREECH
BOOM

ARE YOU BEN? BEN OLIVER?
Huh?!
WHAT?!
GO AWAY!
REESE AND THEM ARE BACK. THEY FOUND A PRISONER, SOME OLD GUY. SAYS HE WANTS TO TALK TO YOU.
TELL REESE TO WAIT.
YOU MISUNDERSTOOD. IT'S THE OLD GUY WANTS TO TALK TO YOU.
TO ME?
THEY GOT A LOT OF QUESTIONS FOR HIM AND HE REFUSES TO SAY A WORD TO ANYONE ELSE. ASKED FOR YOU BY NAME.
HEY. THEY SAID YOU WERE ASKING FOR ME?

IT'S SO GOOD TO SEE YOU.
Uhh... THANK YOU?
YOU LOOK LIKE YOU BEEN THROUGH SOME TOUGH TIMES.
YOU WANT TO TELL ME WHAT HAPPENED?
I NEED YOUR HELP, BEN.
OKAY.
OFFIC
LOOK AT ME.
WHOA!
BEN, IT'S ME.
I DON'T KNOW YOU, MAN. I'M SORRY.
IT'S ME. KYLE.
KYLE REESE.

5
25
evel

WHAT?
I'M YOUR FRIEND, KYLE REESE.
Uhhh, NO. YOU'RE NOT.
I WAS SENT BACK IN TIME.
WERE YOU.
YES. FOR ME THE PRESENT IS MY PAST.
FOR YOUR YOUNG FRIEND KYLE, THE PAST IS HIS FUTURE.
FOR ME, THE FUTURE IS A MYSTERY.
SWELL.

YOU DON'T BELIEVE ME.
NOPE.
IN A FEW WEEKS, JOHN CONNOR WILL SEND YOUR FRIEND KYLE--ME--BACK THROUGH TIME TO 1984. WHERE HE--I--WILL PROTECT SARAH.
SARAH CONNOR.
YES.
AND THEN?
AND THEN I DON'T KNOW.
I'M SURE YOU CAN SEE HOW THAT WEAKENS YOUR STORY.
THE LAST THING I REMEMBER, SARAH AND I WERE RUNNING FROM THE EIGHT HUNDRED. WE WERE IN A FACTORY. I TRIED TO BLOW IT UP. THEN...EVERYTHING WENT BLACK.
WHO TOLD YOU TO SAY ALL THIS?
I WOKE UP IN CAPTIVITY, SURROUNDED BY STRANGERS. THEY WANTED INFORMATION--
OBVIOUSLY REESE WAS INVOLVED, THE PRICK.
--ABOUT THE TIME-DISPLACEMENT TECHNOLOGY. ABOUT THE MACHINES.

SOME TIME AFTER SKYNET ATTACKED, THE MEN WERE REPLACED BY MACHINES AND THE QUESTIONS STARTED TO BE ABOUT THE **RESISTANCE.**
THIS IS LIKE A WHOLE ELABORATE THING.
IT'S TRUE.
OKAY. WELL, I'M GONNA GO NOW.
THIS IS **SERIOUS.** I NEED YOU TO HELP ME, BEN.
I DON'T KNOW WHAT TO TELL YOU, OLD MAN.
I PULLED YOU OUT OF **HELL.** YOU OWE ME.
WE'VE NEVER MET.
YOU'D STILL BE WANDERING ALONE, FEEDING OFF THE DEAD.
SLAM
YOU DON'T **KNOW ME.** DON'T **PRETEND** THAT YOU DO. AND TELL WHOEVER PUT YOU UP TO THIS TO **F*#K HIMSELF.**

BEN!
WHAT'S THAT?
IT'S PROOF.
POST OFFICE

POMONA, CALIFORNIA--
THREE WEEKS LATER
SERGEANT REESE?
YEAH.
JOHN CONNOR IS ASKING FOR YOU. HE WOULD LIKE TO SEE YOU IN THE OPERATIONS ROOM.
CONNOR'S *HERE?*
GOT HERE LAST NIGHT, SIR.

THAT WAS AMAZING. WE SHOULD HAVE BEEN DOING THIS YEARS AGO.
LET'S JUST MAKE SURE WE DO THIS ALWAYS FROM THIS POINT FORWARD.
DEAL.
THERE WILL OF COURSE BE BRIEF INTERLUDES OF FLEEING AND TERROR AND WARFARE.
GOES WITHOUT SAYING.
BUT ALL THE REST OF THE TIME.
YES.
YOU EVER IMAGINE HOW SWEET OUR LIVES WOULD BE IF THERE WAS NEVER ANY SKYNET, ANY MACHINES?
THAT'S TOO DEPRESSING FOR ME. TOO FRUSTRATING.

I DO THINK ABOUT WHAT IT WILL BE LIKE AFTER WE WIN AND THE MACHINES ARE GONE.
AND WHAT'LL IT BE LIKE?
I'M GONNA HAVE A HOUSE WITH A GARDEN. FRESH FRUITS, VEGETABLES. ALL OF 'EM--APPLES, ORANGES, PEARS.
NO PEARS.
YOU'RE RIGHT--SCREW PEARS. PEACHES TOO. BUT WE'LL HAVE BANANAS AND EVERYTHING ELSE.
WHO'S "WE"?
YOU AND ME.
IT'S ALWAYS BEEN YOU AND ME.

YOU CALLED FOR ME, SIR?
REESE. IT'S GOOD TO SEE YOU.
YOU TOO, SIR.
HOW HAVE YOU BEEN?
WE LOST A LOT OF PEOPLE OUT OF PASADENA.
I HEARD. I'M SORRY.
IT WAS UGLY. WE WEREN'T PREPARED FOR THE EIGHT HUNDREDS. YOU SAID THEY'D COME, THAT THEY'D LOOK ***THAT HUMAN*** BUT...
I KNOW. THEY'RE BEYOND IMAGINING.
YEAH.

WE GOT A LOT OF USEFUL INFORMATION OFF THOSE DRIVES YOU STOLE.
WE THINK WE MIGHT BE ABLE TO REPROGRAM AN EIGHT HUNDRED. GIVE IT OBJECTIVES WE CHOOSE.
A TERMINATOR FIGHTING ON OUR SIDE?
WHAT WOULD YOU THINK ABOUT THAT?
AS LONG AS WE'RE FIRING IN THE SAME DIRECTION IT SOUNDS GOOD TO ME.
WE FOUND SOMETHING ELSE TOO. IT HAS TO DO WITH WHY I ASKED YOU HERE.
THERE'S A FACILITY IN LOS ANGELES. IT'S PART OF SKYNET. WE CAPTURED IT A WHILE BACK.
OKAY.
THE TECHNOLOGY WE FOUND INSIDE WE DIDN'T KNOW HOW TO OPERATE UNTIL YOU BROUGHT IN THOSE DRIVES.
NOW THAT WE DO, THERE'S A NEW MISSION... AND WHOEVER WE SEND ISN'T COMING BACK.
THE MISSION IS VITAL TO THE RESISTANCE AND OF PARTICULAR PERSONAL INTEREST TO ME.
I WAS HOPING YOU COULD RECOMMEND A SOLDIER.
SEND ME.

Ughh. I'M TERRIFIED TO SEE WHAT THAT "SURGEON" DID TO ME.
EESH. LOOK AT THAT.
IT'S KIND OF BADASS, ACTUALLY.
BEN? YOU ALL RIGHT?

KYLE?
YOU SAW IT.
HOW IS THIS POSSIBLE?

INSIDE THIS FACILITY THEY FOUND EVIDENCE THAT A T-800 WAS SENT BACK TO 1984 TO KILL SARAH CONNOR.
STOP THE RESISTANCE BEFORE IT STARTS.
I VOLUNTEERED TO GO BACK AND PROTECT HER.
WHEN DOES THIS HAPPEN?
SOON.
JESUS.
I NEED YOUR HELP, BEN.
FOLLOW ME BACK.
WHAT?
FIND ME, SET ME FREE.
WHOEVER HELD ME ALL THESE YEARS, THEY WERE ***INSTRUMENTAL*** IN BUILDING SKYNET.
WE CAN STOP ***ALL THIS*** FROM HAPPENING.

PLEASE. YOU'RE THE ONLY ONE I CAN TRUST WITH THIS.
WHY NOT JUST WARN KYLE?
WE CAN'T INTERFERE WITH HIM AND RISK CHANGING HIS COURSE. HE HAS TO BE FOCUSED ON PROTECTING SARAH.
BEN?
KYLE, I LOVE YOU. YOU SAVED ME FROM A HORRIFYING EXISTENCE, GAVE ME A HOME.
YOU'RE MY BEST FRIEND.
PLEASE, BEN.
I LOVE HER TOO MUCH, KYLE.

JESUS, PAIGE, THAT'S A SICK SCAR.
I KNOW, RIGHT?
WELL, GUYS... END OF THE ROAD.
I'D SAY I WAS GOING TO MISS YOU, BUT YOU TWO HAVE GOTTEN KINDA *GROSS.*
SHUT UP.
DON'T BE GONE TOO LONG, OKAY?
BEN.

THANK YOU. FOR *EVERYTHING.*
TAKE CARE OF EACH OTHER.
YOU READY?
AS I'LL EVER BE.

LOS ANGELES, CALIFORNIA.
DID YOU HOLD ONTO THAT PICTURE I GAVE YOU?
FOR A LONG TIME, YEAH. BUT IT GOT BURNT UP IN A FIREFIGHT ABOUT TEN DAYS AGO.
I JUST WANT TO BE SURE YOU'LL RECOGNIZE HER.
THERE'S NO QUESTION.
WOW.
THAT'S WHAT I SAID TOO.
THANK YOU, KYLE. TO SAY I OWE YOU ONE DOESN'T REALLY COVER IT.
HONESTLY, IT'S AN HONOR.

THERE'S SOMETHING I'VE WANTED TO ASK YOU.
WHY DID YOU VOLUNTEER?
IT'S AN IMPORTANT MISSION, RIGHT?
YEAH.
CAN'T GET SCREWED UP?
THAT'S RIGHT.
FATE OF THE WORLD HANGS IN THE BALANCE?
YEAH.
THEN I'M YOUR GUY.
I'M GLAD I GOT TO KNOW YOU, KYLE.
YOU TOO, JOHN.

IT SUCKS KYLE HAD TO TAKE OFF AGAIN.
YEAH, I'M GONNA MISS HIM.
WHADDYA SAY WE FIND OUT WHO'S GOT THE LIQUOR IN TOWN AND TEACH THEM A LESSON ABOUT PROTECTING THEIR VALUABLES?
Uhh, BEN?
YEAH?
NAKED GUY.
HEY, BUDDY. YOU ALL RIGHT?
I'M LOOKING FOR KYLE REESE.
YOU JUST MISSED HIM.
JOHN CONNOR.

PAIGE, BACK UP.
DO YOU KNOW WHERE JOHN CONNOR IS?
NO IDEA!
WE NEED TO WARN EVERYONE. I THINK THAT WAS AN EIGHT HUNDRED.
A VERY HEALTHY EIGHT HUNDRED.
PAIGE.

OOF!
PAIGE!
NO, NO, NO.
PAIGE.
PAIGE?
NO.

THIS ISN'T RIGHT.
THIS LIFE IS A NIGHTMARE.
MANKIND'S BAD DREAM...
A WORLD BROKEN.
WARPED.
ROTTEN.
WHERE NOTHING IS AS IT WAS MEANT TO BE.

SOMEHOW, SOMEWHERE, THERE WAS A MISSTEP.
SOMETHING SKEWED. TIPPED OFF BALANCE.
WE MADE A MISTAKE AND NOW ALL THE WORLD IS WRONG.
BUT IT'S NOT TOO LATE.
WE CAN PUT IT BACK IN PLACE.
CORRECT IT.
BRING THEM BACK.
I CAN BRING EVERYONE BACK.

THERE'S STILL TIME.
THERE IS HOPE FOR THE FUTURE...
FOR A BETTER WORLD...
...IN THE PAST.
DON'T WORRY, PAIGE.

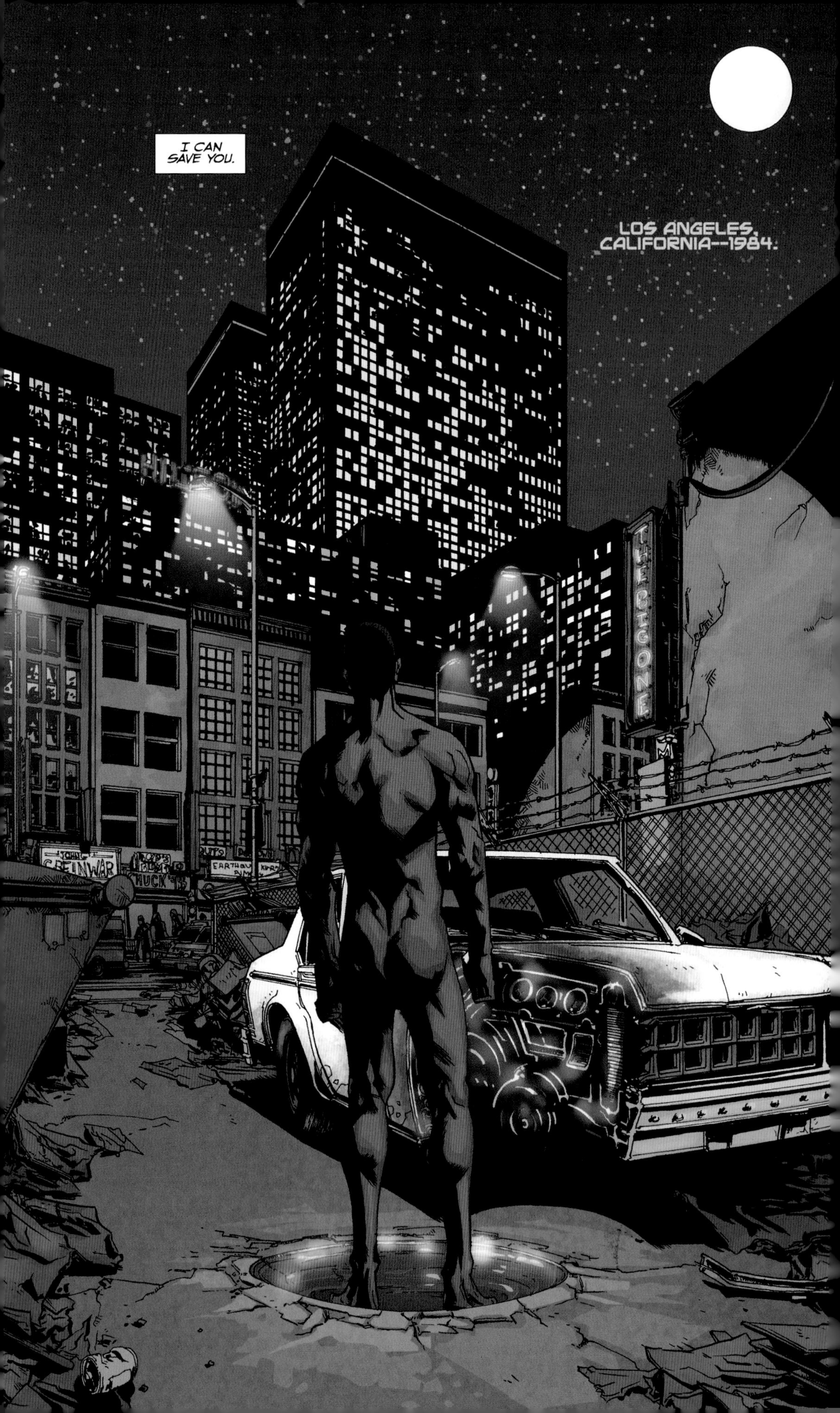
I CAN SAVE YOU.
LOS ANGELES, CALIFORNIA--1984.
THE BIG ONE

SARAH CONNOR
1984

1984

AND WHO WAS THE ENEMY?
A COMPUTER DEFENSE SYSTEM BUILT FOR SAC-NORAD BY **CYBERDYNE SYSTEMS.**
I SEE. AND THIS... **COMPUTER** THINKS IT CAN WIN BY KILLING THE MOTHER OF ITS ENEMY-- KILLING HIM, IN EFFECT, BEFORE HE IS EVEN CONCEIVED? A SORT OF RETROACTIVE ABORTION?
YES.
WHY DIDN'T THE COMPUTER JUST KILL CONNOR THEN? WHY THIS ELABORATE SCHEME WITH THE TERMINATOR?
IT HAD NO CHOICE.
THE DEFENSIVE GRID WAS SMASHED. **WE'D WON.** TAKING OUT CONNOR THEN WOULD MAKE NO DIFFERENCE. SKYNET HAD TO WIPE OUT HIS ENTIRE EXISTENCE.
IS THAT WHEN YOU CAPTURED THE LAB COMPLEX AND FOUND THAT...WHAT WAS IT CALLED...THE TIME-DISPLACEMENT EQUIPMENT?
THAT'S RIGHT. THE TERMINATOR HAD ALREADY GONE THROUGH. CONNOR SENT ME TO INTERCEPT, THEN THEY BLEW THE WHOLE PLACE.
WELL, HOW ARE YOU SUPPOSED TO GET BACK?
I CAN'T.
NOBODY GOES HOME. NOBODY ELSE COMES THROUGH.
IT'S JUST HIM...
...AND ME.
YOU CAN STOP IT THERE.

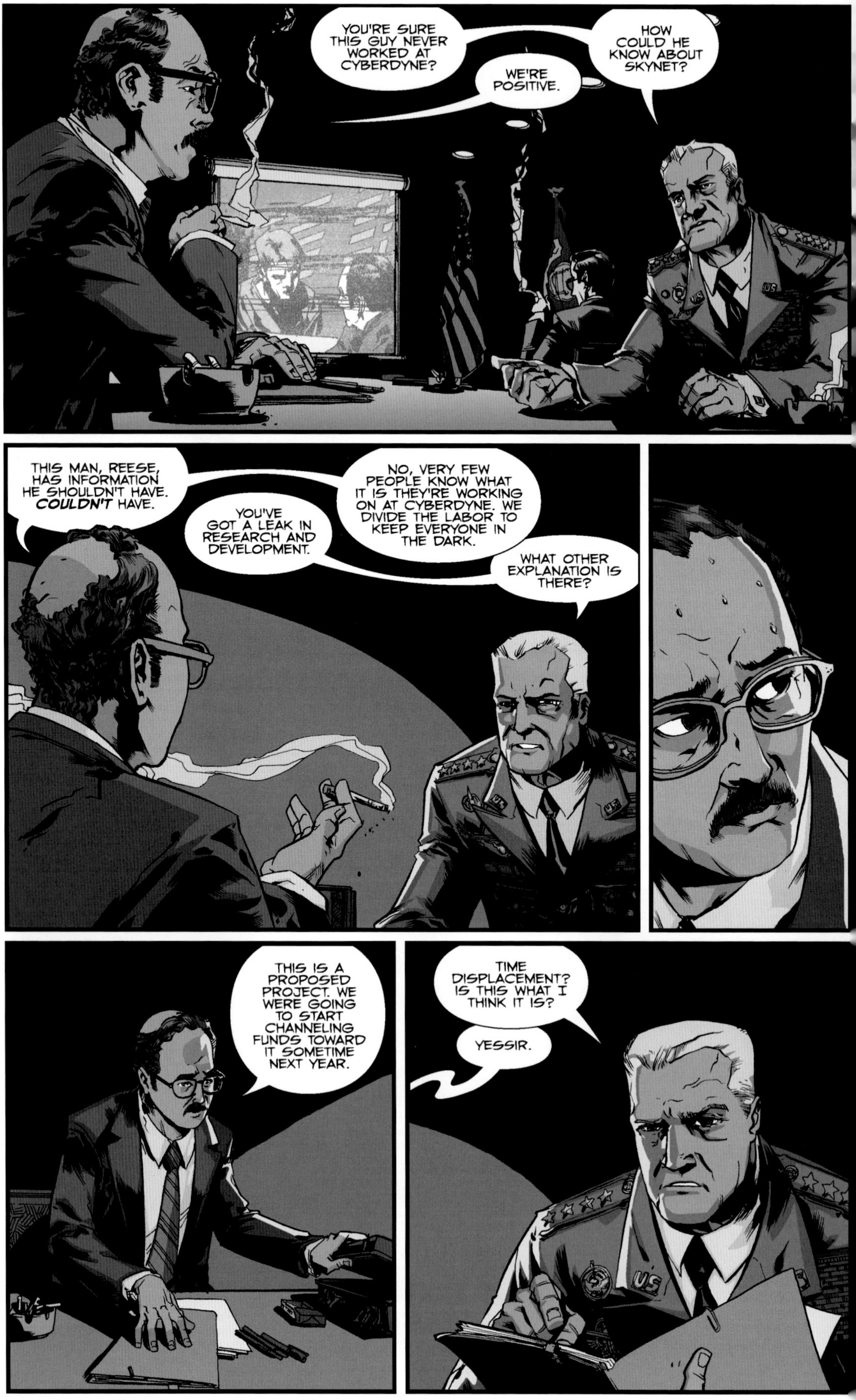
YOU'RE SURE THIS GUY NEVER WORKED AT CYBERDYNE?
WE'RE POSITIVE.
HOW COULD HE KNOW ABOUT SKYNET?
THIS MAN, REESE, HAS INFORMATION HE SHOULDN'T HAVE. COULDN'T HAVE.
YOU'VE GOT A LEAK IN RESEARCH AND DEVELOPMENT.
NO, VERY FEW PEOPLE KNOW WHAT IT IS THEY'RE WORKING ON AT CYBERDYNE. WE DIVIDE THE LABOR TO KEEP EVERYONE IN THE DARK.
WHAT OTHER EXPLANATION IS THERE?
THIS IS A PROPOSED PROJECT. WE WERE GOING TO START CHANNELING FUNDS TOWARD IT SOMETIME NEXT YEAR.
TIME DISPLACEMENT? IS THIS WHAT I THINK IT IS?
YESSIR.

THIS ISN'T SCIENCE FICTION?
IT IS RIGHT NOW. BUT WE WERE PLANNING ON PUTTING FIVE HUNDRED MILLION INTO THIS PROJECT THE FIRST YEAR ALONE. FORTY YEARS FROM NOW, WHO KNOWS.
WE NEED TO CONSIDER THE POSSIBILITY, AS IMPLAUSIBLE AS IT SOUNDS, THAT KYLE REESE IS TELLING THE TRUTH.
HIS VALUE COULD BE IMMEASURABLE TO US. NOT TO MENTION THE MACHINE ITSELF.
HE'S BEING HELD BY THE L.A.P.D.?
HE ESCAPED LATE LAST NIGHT. SOMEONE OR SOMETHING CAME IN AND BLEW THE PLACE TO HELL. KILLED EVERYONE INSIDE. REESE'S BODY WASN'T RECOVERED.
LET'S FIND HIM AND BRING HIM IN. A BLACK SITE. I DON'T WANT ANY INTERFERENCE.
ROLL IT BACK.
NOBODY GOES HOME. NOBODY ELSE COMES THROUGH.
IT'S JUST HIM...
...AND ME.

TWENTY-SIX HOURS EARLIER.
YOU SHOULD SEE THIS PLACE, PAIGE.

IT'S UNBELIEVABLE.
DAMMIT.
amega
THEY HAVE SO MUCH OF EVERYTHING.
Quik·LENS
DAMMIT.
THERE THEY ARE.
ANYTHING YOU CAN THINK OF, IT'S HERE IN ABUNDANCE.
MEN'S FORMAL
Calistan Carpets
modern living

IT'S BEAUTIFUL, BUT IT'S CRAZY TOO.
PEEPSHOW
BIZARRE.
EGGPLANT 39¢ lb.
I WATCHED A GUY THROW AWAY A HUGE BAG OF HOT FOOD. HE JUST THREW IT OUT. GOD KNOWS WHY.
IT WAS DELICIOUS.

BUT THE CRAZIEST THING?
THERE ARE PEOPLE...
...EVERYWHERE.
YOU'VE NEVER SEEN SO MANY PEOPLE. JUST WALKING AROUND. HAPPY. SAFE. THEY'RE NOT AFRAID LIKE WE ARE.
ALL THIS TIME I HAD AN IDEA OF WHAT WE WERE FIGHTING FOR, BUT I NEVER REALLY KNEW. NOT UNTIL NOW.
WE'VE GOT TO SAVE IT.
I'VE GOT TO FIND KYLE.

THE OLD GUY TOLD ME WHEN HE GOT TO 1984 HE WAS ABLE TO FIND SARAH CONNOR, TELL HER ABOUT THE FUTURE.
THIRTY-SIX HOURS LATER.
BUT THE TERMINATOR CAUGHT UP WITH THEM...
VROOM
...HUNTED THEM DOWN.

HE SAID IT CHASED THEM TO A FACTORY NEAR DOWNTOWN.
DON'T STOP! RUN!
SHNK
THAT THERE WAS A BIG EXPLOSION.
BOOM

I'LL BE READY.
SKREEE

MR. CORT?
JUST INTERCEPTED A 911 CALL. COUPLE OF TRUCKERS SAID THEY HAD THEIR TANKER STOLEN BY A MAN WITH A...METAL FACE.
WHERE?
THE TWO HUNDRED BLOCK OF SOUTH GRAND. DOWNTOWN.
LET'S MOVE. TELL THE TEAM WE WANT THE MACHINE AND REESE. IN THAT ORDER.

Oh NO...
AHH!

SLAM
YOU'RE TERMINATED, F%#@ER.

clik
ZZZZZT
LOS ANGELES
MEDICAL

GO GO GO!

PULSE IS WEAK.
MY LEG...
DAMMIT.

COLLECT THE SPECIMEN. GET EVERYTHING.
YESSIR.
WHERE'S REESE?
IS HE ALIVE?
BARELY, SIR.
BAG HIM.

SARAH...
KYLE.

SARAH CONNOR...
SLAM

Oh MY GOD, PAIGE-- I KNOW THIS PLACE.
THIS IS WHERE WE...

I CAN'T DO THIS ALONE.
I'M GOING TO NEED HELP.

BORRADO, MEXICO.
FOUR MONTHS LATER.
PTOO
HEY, SARAH!
FOUND THIS GUY IN TOWN. HE WAS ASKING ABOUT YOU.

WHO ARE YOU?
MY NAME IS BEN.
WHAT DO YOU WANT, BEN?
I NEED YOUR HELP.
I'M A FRIEND OF KYLE REESE. I HAVE REASON TO BELIEVE HE'S STILL ALIVE.
LET HIM GO, RAMON. I CAN HANDLE IT.
KYLE? ALIVE?
I FOLLOWED KYLE HERE FROM THE YEAR 2029.
AFTER THE EXPLOSION AT THE FACTORY, I WATCHED HIS BODY GET TAKEN TO A SECURE FACILITY.

I BELIEVE HE'S BEING HELD THERE, BUT I CAN'T GET HIM OUT BY MYSELF...
HEY, WHERE ARE YOU GOING?

I'M GOING TO GET A LOT OF GUNS.

BOMBS AWAY!
SMASH
DO YOU SEE THAT?
WHOA!!
WHAT THE HELL?!

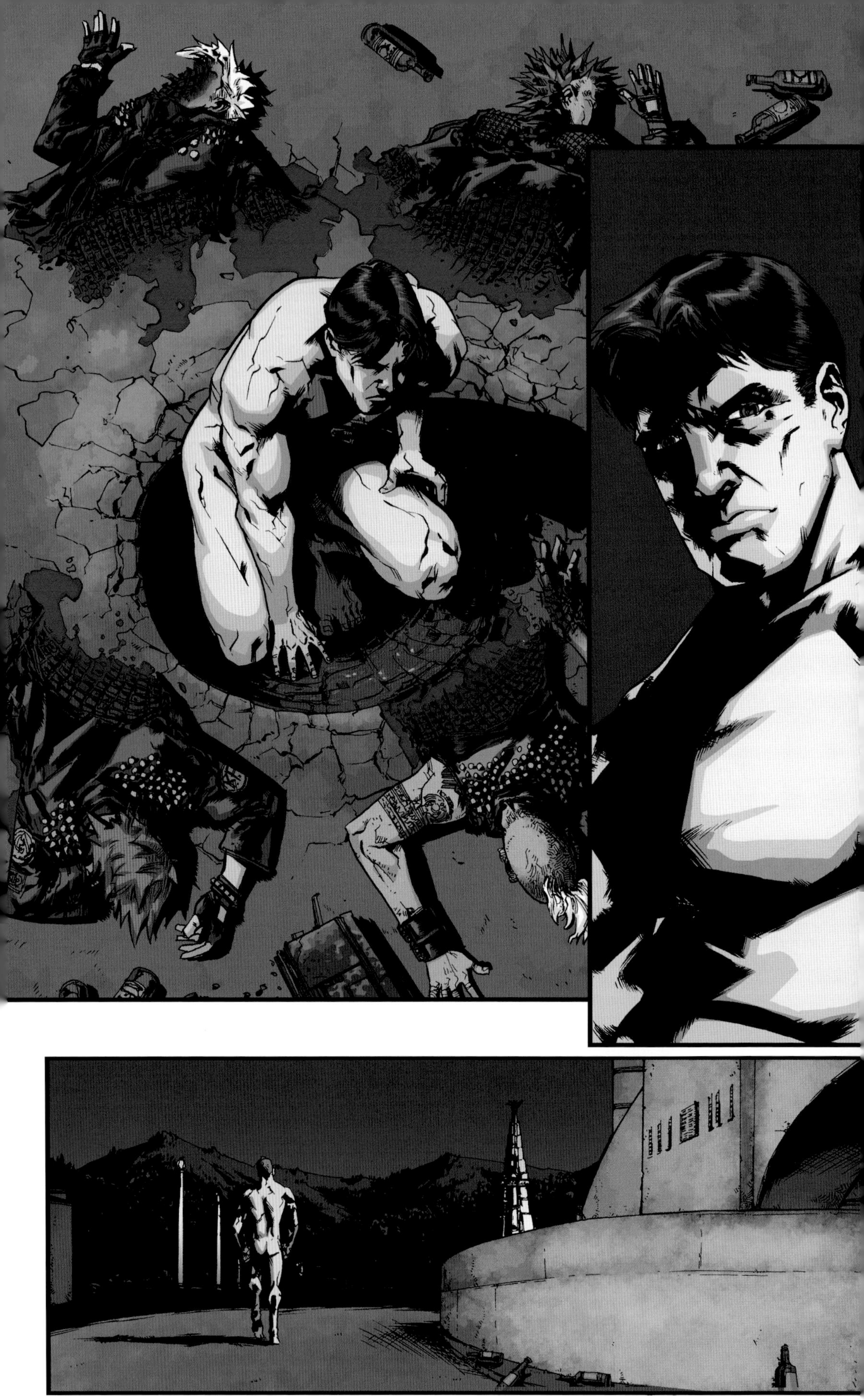

U.S. / MEXICO BORDER.
HUAAAA!
PTTT
Ugghh.

SARAH? QUICK QUESTION.
ARE YOU *PREGNANT?*
FOUR AND A HALF MONTHS.

Oh MY GOD.
KYLE? KYLE IS THE FATHER?
I KNOW IT MUST BE HARD TO WRAP YOUR HEAD AROUND.
THAT FREAKY, TIME-TRAVELING...
WHERE ARE YOU GOING?
I'M TAKING YOU BACK.
WHAT?
THERE'S NO WAY I'M TAKING YOU ON THIS MISSION WHEN YOU'VE GOT THE LEADER OF THE RESISTANCE IN YOUR BELLY.
BEN?
WHAT?!

Oh...
I MET THE LOVE OF MY LIFE...THE FATHER OF MY UNBORN CHILD, AND THIRTY-SIX HOURS LATER HE WAS DEAD.
OR AT LEAST I THOUGHT HE WAS. NOW I LEARN HE'S ALIVE AND BEING HELD PRISONER.
IF YOU THINK FOR A **SECOND** THAT THERE IS ANYTHING ON THIS EARTH THAT CAN KEEP ME FROM FINDING HIM ***NOW,*** YOU'RE OUT OF YOUR F*$#ING MIND.
I'D LOVE TO HAVE YOUR HELP, BUT I'M GOING EITHER WAY.
WHAT'S IT GONNA BE, BEN?

JESUS!
LONG NIGHT, BUDDY?
HEY!!
SHRAK
KRNCH
VROOM

Huh?
Psst.
CRAK
Guhh...

WHA--?!

BLAM
SARAH?
YOU'RE ALIVE, THAN GOD.
THEY TOLD ME YOU WERE **DEAD.**
I WAS AFRAID I'D **NEVER** SEE YOU AGAIN
I'M SO HAPPY I FOUND YOU.
THERE'S SOMETHING I NEED TO TELL YOU.
WAIT. **BEN?**

WHAT THE HELL ARE YOU DOING HERE?
IT'S A LONG STORY. RIGHT NOW I SUGGEST WE GET OUT OF HERE.
IN HERE!

Oh GOD.
STUPID BASTARDS...
THEY'RE PUTTING IT BACK TOGETHER.
YOU GUYS GO AHEAD. I'LL CATCH UP.

BLAM
BLAM
AHH!
BEN! HURRY UP, GET IN!
SKREEECH

Oh GOD...
RUN!!!
BOOM
KYLE, I CAN'T BELIEVE YOU'RE ALIVE.
YOU SHOULDN'T HAVE COME FOR ME. IT WAS STUPID. IT WAS DANGEROUS. YOU'RE TOO IMPORTANT.

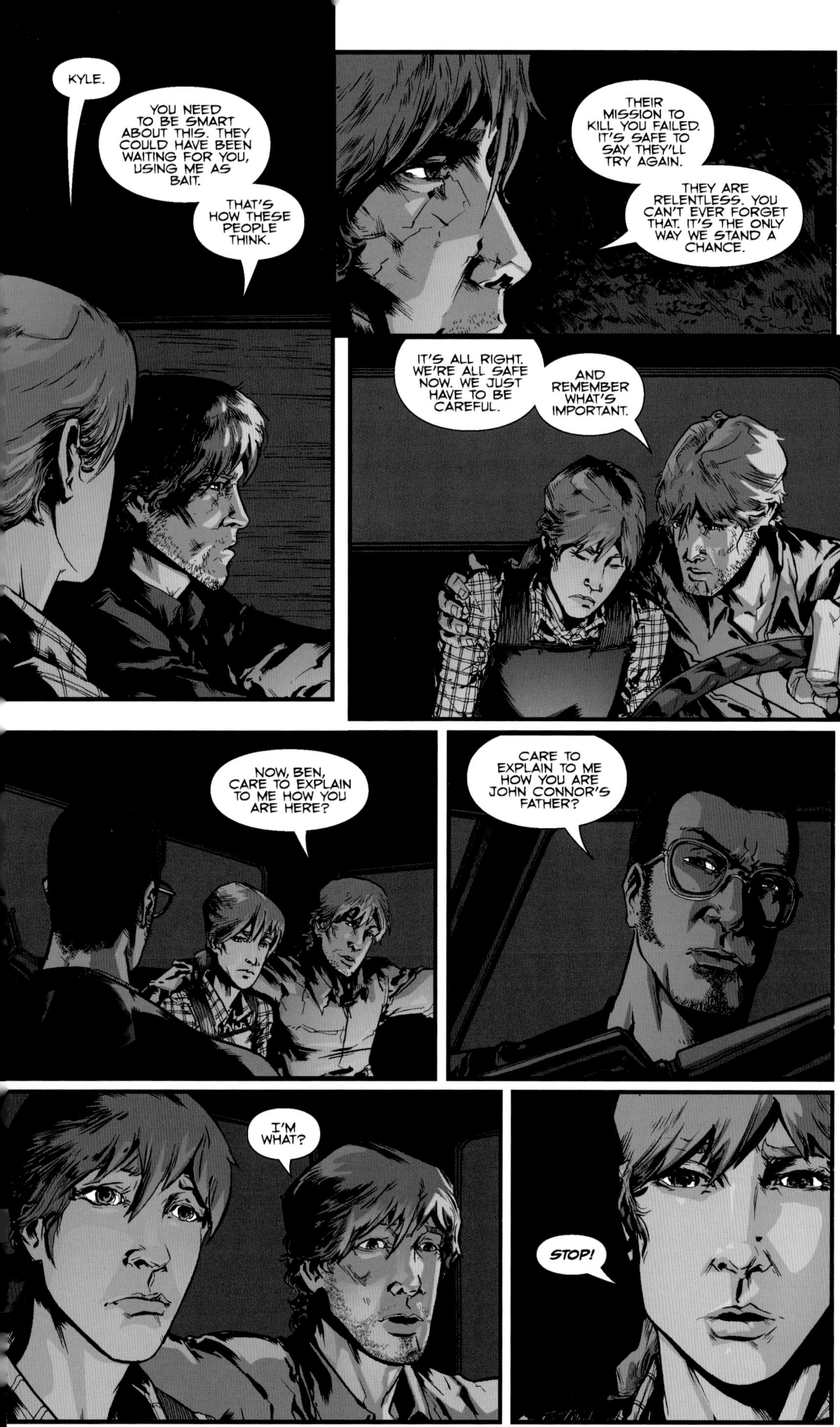
KYLE.
YOU NEED TO BE SMART ABOUT THIS. THEY COULD HAVE BEEN WAITING FOR YOU, USING ME AS BAIT.
THAT'S HOW THESE PEOPLE THINK.
THEIR MISSION TO KILL YOU FAILED. IT'S SAFE TO SAY THEY'LL TRY AGAIN.
THEY ARE RELENTLESS. YOU CAN'T EVER FORGET THAT. IT'S THE ONLY WAY WE STAND A CHANCE.
IT'S ALL RIGHT. WE'RE ALL SAFE NOW. WE JUST HAVE TO BE CAREFUL.
AND REMEMBER WHAT'S IMPORTANT.
NOW, BEN, CARE TO EXPLAIN TO ME HOW YOU ARE HERE?
CARE TO EXPLAIN TO ME HOW YOU ARE JOHN CONNOR'S FATHER?
I'M WHAT?
STOP!

SKREECH
SARAH CONNOR.
S*#T.
BRAKKA BRAKKA BRAKKA
SCREEEEEE

DEAD END
BLAM BLAM
BLAM BLAM BLAM
AHH!
SMASH
CONSTRUCTION SITE DO NOT ENTER
HOLD ON!

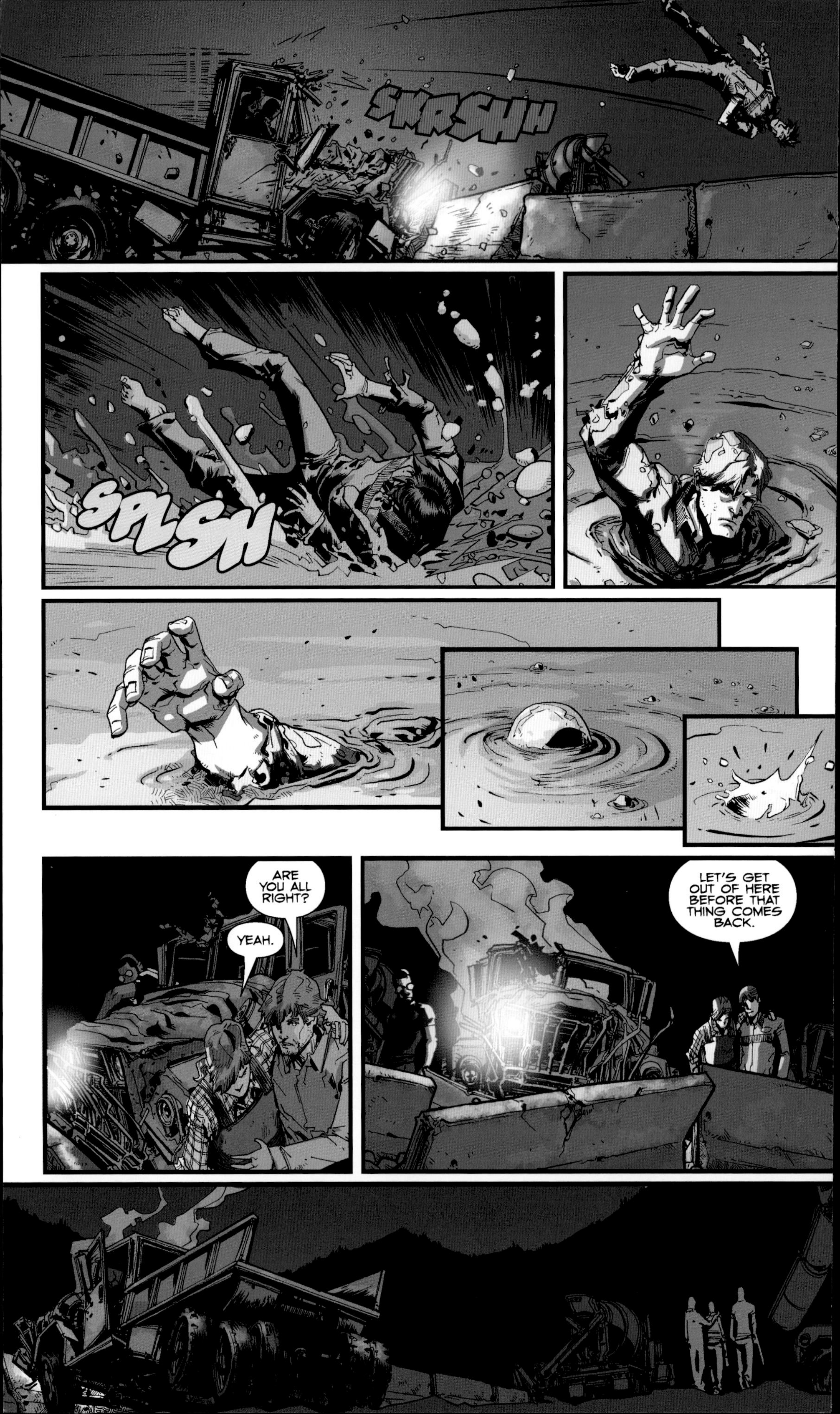
SKRSHH
SPLSH
ARE YOU ALL RIGHT?
YEAH.
LET'S GET OUT OF HERE BEFORE THAT THING COMES BACK.

MR. CORT?
WERE YOU ABLE TO RECOVER ANYTHING?
YES, BUT NOT MUCH, SIR. MOST OF IT WAS BLOWN TO SCRAP.
SHOW ME.
THIS IS IT?
I'M AFRAID SO, SIR.

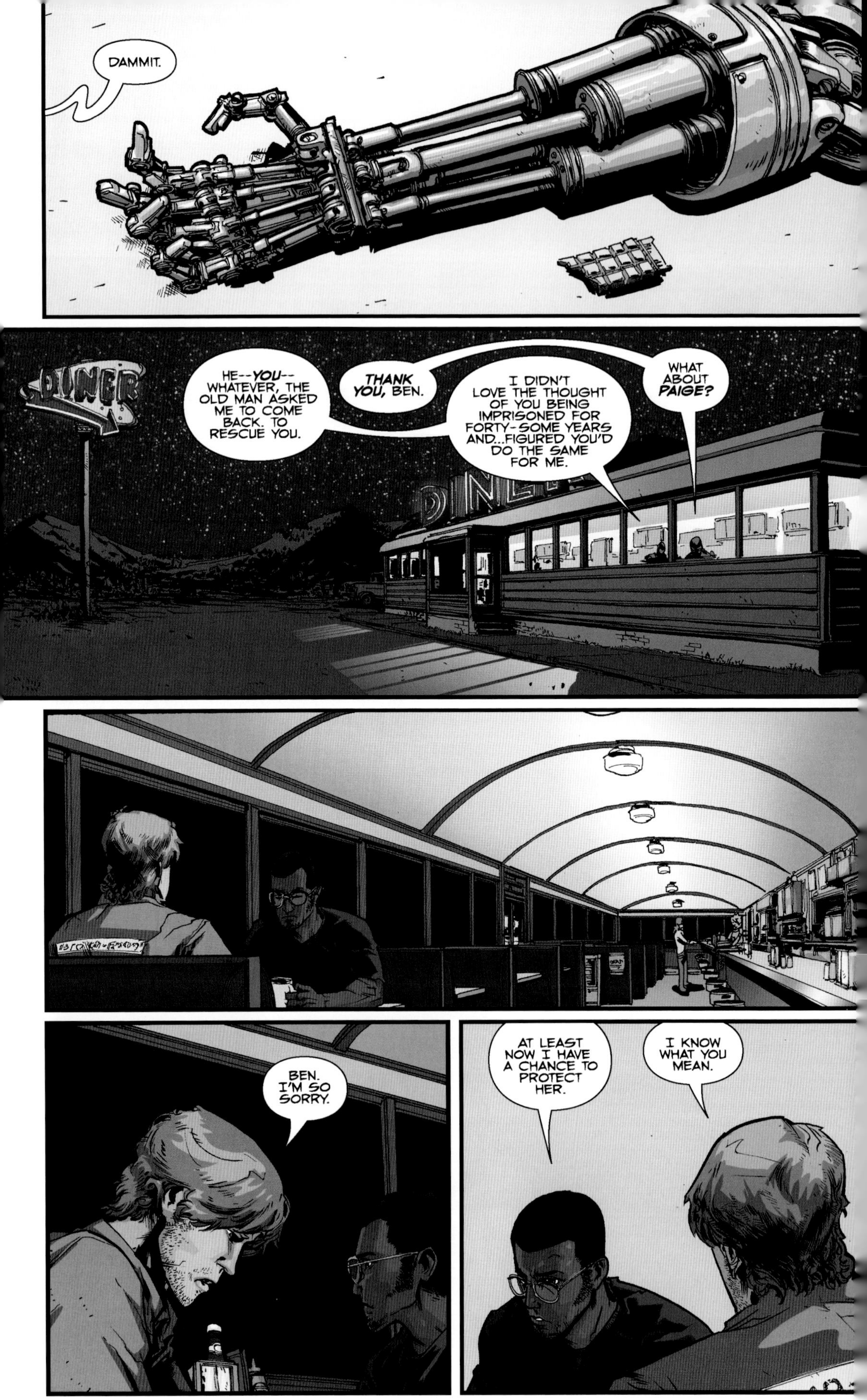
DAMMIT.
HE--YOU--WHATEVER, THE OLD MAN ASKED ME TO COME BACK. TO RESCUE YOU.
THANK YOU, BEN.
I DIDN'T LOVE THE THOUGHT OF YOU BEING IMPRISONED FOR FORTY-SOME YEARS AND...FIGURED YOU'D DO THE SAME FOR ME.
WHAT ABOUT PAIGE?
DINER
BEN. I'M SO SORRY.
AT LEAST NOW I HAVE A CHANCE TO PROTECT HER.
I KNOW WHAT YOU MEAN.

HONESTLY, THAT'S REALLY WHY I CAME BACK. TO SAVE PAIGE. YOU NEED SOMETHING TO WORK TOWARD, TO LOOK FORWARD TO.
CAN'T LIVE IN THE PAST.
BEN...
YOU KNOW WHAT I MEAN.
GOT ANY NAMES PICKED OUT?
JOHN.
Best
IN TOWN
CALL AGAIN
Sorry no Checks
NO KIDDIN'. MY FATHER'S NAME WAS JOHN. WHAT MADE YOU CHOOSE IT?
IN ANOTHER LIFE I MIGHT HAVE BEEN ABLE TO TELL YOU, BUT IN THIS ONE...
...IT'S JUST HIS NAME.
ALL THE CONVERSATIONS I HAD WITH JOHN CONNOR AND I NEVER KNEW...
YOU THINK HE DID?
I DON'T KNOW. I DON'T KNOW HOW ANY OF THIS IS EVEN ***POSSIBLE.***
I CAN SEE IT.
WHAT DO YOU MEAN?
THE WAY JOHN CONNOR IS, THE WAY YOU ARE. IT MAKES SENSE YOU'RE HIS DAD.
DOES IT? I WAS SENT TO PROTECT SARAH, NOT TO...YOU KNOW.
SO?

WHAT'RE YOU GUYS TALKING ABOUT?
TIME-TRAVELING DADDIES.
I WAS JUST SAYING WE DON'T KNOW WHAT THE EFFECTS OF OUR ACTIONS ARE HERE.
I WAS SUPPOSED TO BE HELD PRISONER FOR FORTY-FIVE YEARS IN THAT PLACE. NOW I'M FREE. WHAT IF THAT MESSES SOMETHING UP?
YOU'RE WORRIED ABOUT SCREWING UP THE FUTURE?
YEAH.
THEN YOU'RE AN *IDIOT.*
THE FUTURE IS A WASTELAND. SCORCHED EARTH. BODIES EVERYWHERE. A MISERABLE PLACE OF CONSTANT DANGER WHERE EVERYONE YOU LOVE *DIES.*
PRETTY MUCH ANY CHANGE AT ALL IS GONNA BE AN IMPROVEMENT.
FAIR POINT.
WELL, THEN LET'S *CHANGE* IT. LET'S BE *PREPARED.*
WHAT DO YOU MEAN?
HOW DOES THE RESISTANCE BEGIN?
YOU WOULD KNOW BETTER THAN ME.
WHY?
'CAUSE YOU STARTED IT.

OKAY THEN, LET'S START IT.
RIGHT NOW.
IN THIS DINER IN THE MIDDLE OF GOD KNOWS WHERE, LET'S FORM THE RESISTANCE.
ALL RIGHT.
TO THE RESISTANCE!
THIS IS GOOD. WE'RE GETTING A HEAD START.
SPEAKING OF WHICH, WE SHOULD PROBABLY HEAD OUT.
THAT THING WILL BE COMING FOR US.
DINER
THE FEDS WILL TOO. THEY DON'T TAKE KINDLY TO PEOPLE BLOWING UP THEIR ARMY BASES.
GOT ANY PLACE IN MIND?
YEAH...

THREE WEEKS LATER.
RRRMMMBLL
RUN!
CRAK
SKRASH

GAHH!
BORRADO, MEXICO.
FIVE MONTHS LATER.
...JESUS.
YOU ALL RIGHT?
BAD DREAM.
WANT A STRAWBERRY?
THAT EIGHT HUNDRED WAS COMING FOR US OR...FOR YOU. FOR YOU AND JOHN.
JUST A DREAM.

IT'S NOT JUST A DREAM, SARAH. THEY'LL ALWAYS BE COMING FOR YOU.
C'MON, LET'S WORK ON HAND-TO-HAND.
SARAH.
I'M IN THE MIDDLE OF SOMETHING.
THIS IS MORE IMPORTANT.
IT'S NOT MORE IMPORTANT, KYLE.

YES IT IS!
UGGH.
NO, KYLE, IT'S **NOT.** PICKING STRAWBERRIES IS IMPORTANT TOO. LIVING LIFE IS IMPORTANT.
THERE'S A WORLD WHERE WE HAVE NONE OF THIS TIME. IF IT WEREN'T FOR BEN YOU'D BE LOCKED IN A CELL BEING TORTURED RIGHT NOW AND I'D THINK YOU WERE DEAD.
THIS TIME IS A GIFT. IF WE'RE GOING TO SPEND IT ALL THROWING PUNCHES AT EACH OTHER, WHAT'S THE POINT?
KYLE?

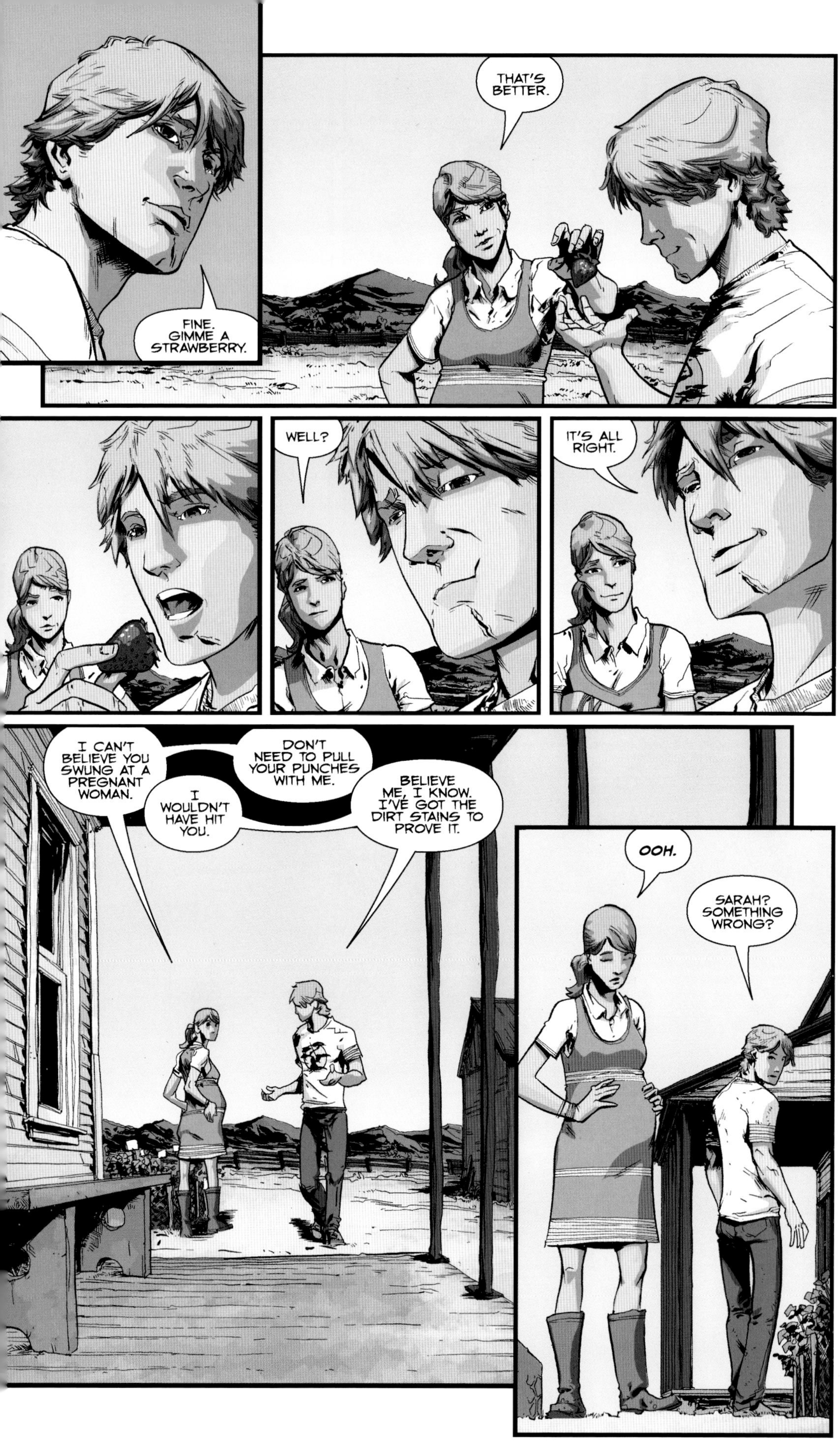

FINE. GIMME A STRAWBERRY.
THAT'S BETTER.
WELL?
IT'S ALL RIGHT.
I CAN'T BELIEVE YOU SWUNG AT A PREGNANT WOMAN.
I WOULDN'T HAVE HIT YOU.
DON'T NEED TO PULL YOUR PUNCHES WITH ME.
BELIEVE ME, I KNOW. I'VE GOT THE DIRT STAINS TO PROVE IT.
OOH.
SARAH? SOMETHING WRONG?

AHHH!
VINCE AND CARLO WENT TO TOWN TO GET A DOCTOR. THEY SHOULDN'T BE TOO LONG.
YOU'RE OKAY, YOU'RE OKAY.
I AM NOT OKAY.
YOU'RE... GOING TO BE?
GRRR
GRRR
KYLE!
THE DOGS ARE GOING CRAZY.
WHAT?!
Oh NO.

I'M LOOKING FOR SARAH CONNOR.
SNAP
STAY THE F*#K BACK!
GET SARAH IN THE CAR AND DRIVE. JUST KEEP DRIVING.
GET AS FAR AWAY AS POSSIBLE.
KYLE!
YOU'RE GOING TO BE OKAY.
I LOVE YOU.
KYLE, NO, COME WITH US.
BRAKKA BRAKKA

GAHHH!
SARAH, COME ON!
BBRAP
BRAKKA BRAKKA
AHH!

BEN, STOP THE CAR!
NO! WHY?
NOW!
WHAT'S THE MATTER?

I NEED YOU TO DELIVER THIS BABY.
I...
YOU'RE GOING TO DO THIS AND YOU'RE GONNA DO IT REALLY F*$#@*G WELL, YOU HEAR ME?
SMASH

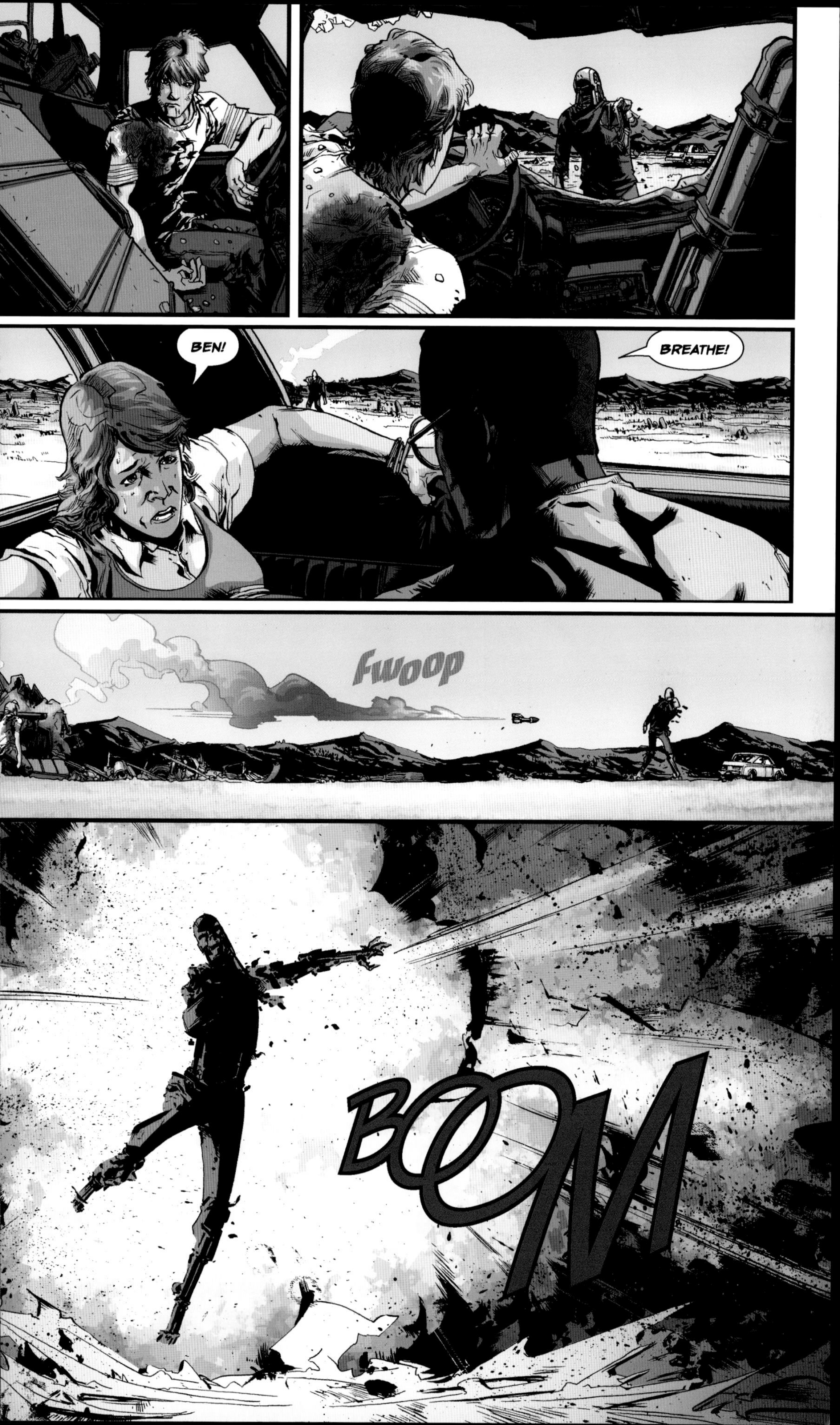
BEN!
BREATHE!
FWOOP
BOOM

WHAT WAS THAT?
NOTHING! I DON'T KNOW! I'M SEEING CRAZY THINGS RIGHT NOW!
GAHHH!
OH MY GOD.
OH MY GOD.

KYLE...
SMASH

KRUNNCH
KYLE!

KYLE, HOLD ON...
STAY HIDDEN, STAY PREPARED. TEACH JOHN THE SAME.
YOU CAN TEACH HIM.
SARAH...
THE MOST IMPORTANT THING IS THAT YOU STAY OUT OF SIGHT. IF THEY FIND YOU, IF THEY KNOW WHERE JOHN IS, THEY'LL SEND MORE BACK.
HE NEEDS A FATHER. HE NEEDS YOU, KYLE.
IT ONLY MATTERS WHO HIS MOTHER IS.

I NEED YOU, KYLE.
NO, YOU DON'T. YOU'RE STRONG, SARAH. YOU'RE STRONGER THAN I EVER COULD HAVE IMAGINED.
BEN...
THANK YOU...
KYLE!
LET ME SEE JOHN.

KEEP HIM SAFE...
KEEP HIM SAFE...
KEEP HIM SAFE...

KYLE

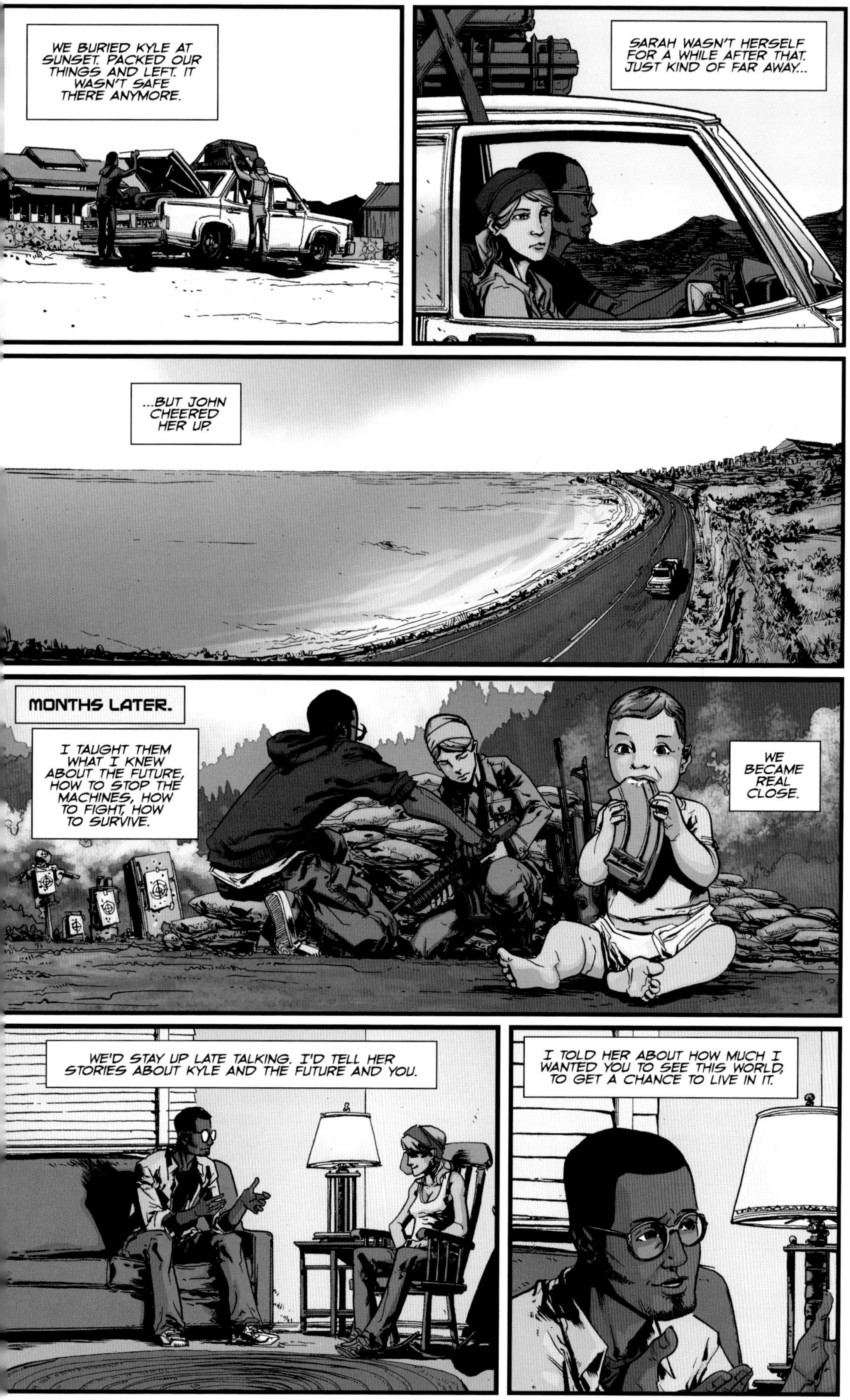
WE BURIED KYLE AT SUNSET. PACKED OUR THINGS AND LEFT. IT WASN'T SAFE THERE ANYMORE.
SARAH WASN'T HERSELF FOR A WHILE AFTER THAT. JUST KIND OF FAR AWAY...
...BUT JOHN CHEERED HER UP.
MONTHS LATER.
I TAUGHT THEM WHAT I KNEW ABOUT THE FUTURE, HOW TO STOP THE MACHINES, HOW TO FIGHT, HOW TO SURVIVE.
WE BECAME REAL CLOSE.
WE'D STAY UP LATE TALKING. I'D TELL HER STORIES ABOUT KYLE AND THE FUTURE AND YOU.
I TOLD HER ABOUT HOW MUCH I WANTED YOU TO SEE THIS WORLD, TO GET A CHANCE TO LIVE IN IT.

SHE'D CRY THINKING ABOUT JOHN LIVING IN THE WORLD OF THE MACHINES.
WE AGREED WE HAD TO STOP IT. THAT WE COULDN'T JUST PREPARE FOR THE FUTURE-- WE HAD TO FIGHT IT.
STOP IT FROM COMING AT ALL.
WE DID WHAT WE COULD.
RAVEN TECHNOLOGIES
BOOM
BUT WE BOTH KNEW, SOMEWHERE IN THE BACK OF OUR MINDS, THAT THERE WOULD ALWAYS BE PEOPLE FIGHTING IN THE OPPOSITE DIRECTION...

...FORCING THE FUTURE, PUSHING OUR TECHNOLOGY TO THE BREAKING POINT.
WE PUT TOGETHER THIS COMPOSITE IMAGE FROM NOTES WE MADE ON THE SPECIMEN, BEFORE IT WAS DESTROYED.
AND YOU CAN BUILD IT?
THE HARDWARE IS INCREDIBLY COMPLEX, BUT WE CAN REPLICATE IT, GIVEN TIME. IT'S THE SOFTWARE THAT'S BEYOND OUR... IMMEDIATE GRASP.
HOW FAR BEYOND?
DECADES.
WE DID PICK UP A RADIATION SIGNATURE SIMILAR TO WHAT WE FOUND IN THE FACTORY.
WHERE?
MIDDLE OF NOWHERE, MEXICO.
...HUMANS WILL ALWAYS FIGHT FOR PROGRESS. THEY'LL HURTLE THEMSELVES FORWARD REGARDLESS OF WHAT LIES AHEAD.
SEND A RECOVERY TEAM. BRING WHATEVER THEY FIND DIRECTLY TO ME.
YES, SIR.
IT'S NOT THAT WE'RE EVIL OR HEARTLESS. IT'S JUST OUR NATURE.

I'D LEAVE FROM TIME TO TIME, GO UP NORTH TO CHECK ON YOUR PARENTS, MAKE SURE THEY WERE SAFE.
THEY WERE SO GOOD TO ME BACK IN THE DAY. TAKING CARE OF ME WHEN I WAS NEW TO THE COLONY AND ALL ALONE.
FEEDING ME, CARING FOR ME... FORCING YOU TO HANG OUT WITH ME.
I FOUND YOUR MOM COMING OUT OF SCHOOL WITH HER FRIENDS. SHE WAS HAPPY.
SHE LOOKED JUST LIKE YOU, PAIGE.
IT REMINDED ME OF WHY I'M HERE.

I DON'T KNOW WHEN TO GIVE THIS TO YOU, WHEN TO WARN YOU...MAYBE WE'LL STOP THE WAR FROM EVER COMING AND I WON'T EVER HAVE TO...
I don't know when to give this to you, when to warn you... Maybe we'll stop the war from ever coming and I won't ever have to
...EITHER WAY, WE'LL BE TOGETHER.
AND WE'LL LIVE.
VROOM-VROOM!
HEY, BUDDY. WANNA LEARN HOW TO HOTWIRE A CAR?

BEN!
BEN?
HI, SARAH.
WELCOME HOME.
MAYBE I'M CRAZY BUT TO ME, RIGHT NOW...
THE FUTURE LOOKS BRIGHT.
THE END

DESIGNING THE TERMINATOR

Art by Andy MacDonald

Andy MacDonald and Dan Jackson's tryout illustration. Needless to say, it got them both the gig. The line art was later used as the cover for the Dark Horse 100 limited edition of *Terminator: 2029* #1.

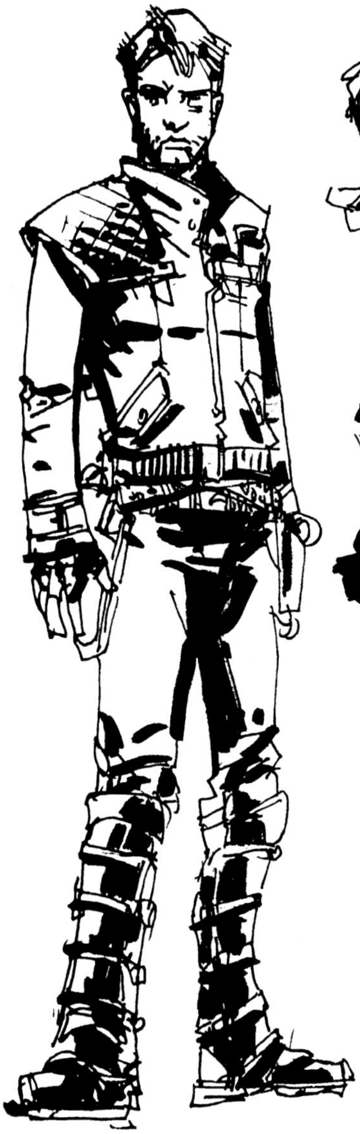

KYLE REESE

OUR FIRST LOOK AT ZACK'S CREATION—THE TROUBLED, TOUGH, HILARIOUS BEN.

BEN AND PAIGE GEARED UP AND READY FOR ACTION.

LEADER OF THE RESISTANCE,
JOHN CONNOR.

SARAH CONNOR

THE VILLAINS—(CLOCKWISE FROM LEFT) CORT, BAKER, AND THE GENERAL.

RED

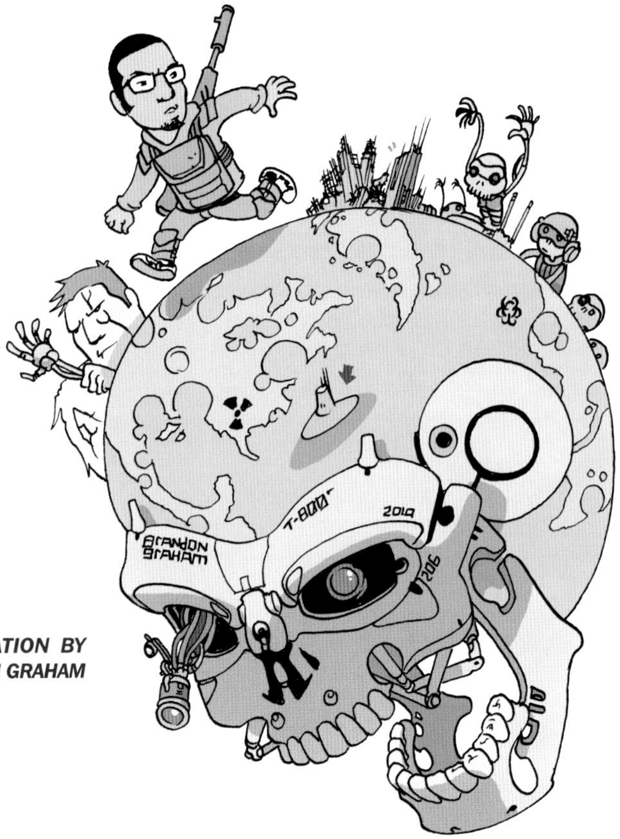

ILLUSTRATION BY BRANDON GRAHAM

ILLUSTRATION BY ANDY MACDONALD

RECOMMENDED DARK HORSE READING . . .

DR. HORRIBLE AND OTHER HORRIBLE STORIES

Zack Whedon, Eric Canete, Farel Dalrymple, Jim Rugg, Joëlle Jones, and Scott Hepburn

From the smash-hit web musical *Dr. Horrible's Sing-Along Blog* come the earliest tales in the lives of Dr. Horrible, Captain Hammer, Penny, Moist, and the upper echelon of all things awful, the Evil League of Evil.

ISBN 978-1-59582-577-3 $9.99

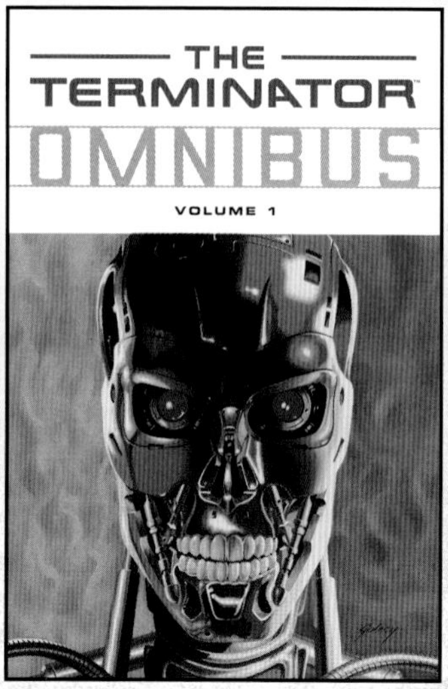

THE TERMINATOR OMNIBUS Volume 1

James Robinson, John Arcudi, Matt Wagner, Guy Davis, and more

They came from another time to ensure that the future would belong solely to the machines. They are Terminators—indestructible killing engines hiding inside shells of flesh and blood. Tireless, fearless, merciless, unencumbered by human emotion, dedicated to the complete eradication of mankind.

978-1-59307-916-1 $24.99

SERENITY: THE SHEPHERD'S TALE

Joss Whedon, Zack Whedon, and Chris Samnee

Who was Shepherd Book before meeting the *Serenity* crew, how did he become their trusted ally, and how did he find God in a bowl of soup? Answers to these and more questions are uncovered in this original graphic novel.

ISBN 978-1-59582-561-2 $14.99

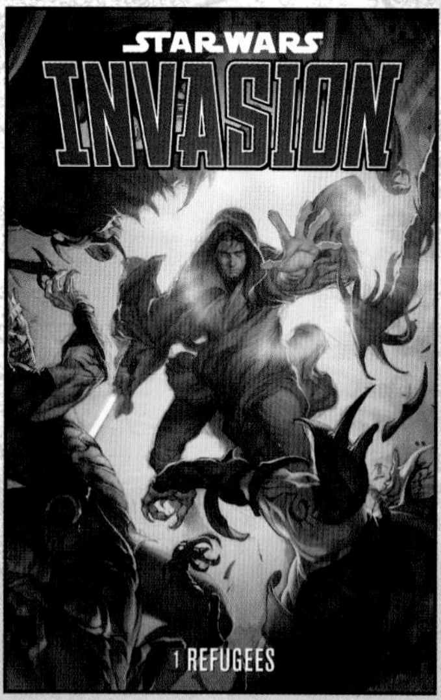

STAR WARS: INVASION Volume 1—Refugees

Tom Taylor, Colin Wilson

Twenty-five years after the Battle of Yavin, Luke Skywalker and the galaxy are facing their first real threat since the Sith were defeated: an invasion of hostile warriors from another galaxy—the Yuuzhan Vong!

978-1-59582-479-0 $18.99

DARK HORSE BOOKS

AVAILABLE AT YOUR LOCAL COMICS SHOP OR BOOKSTORE

To find a comics shop in your area, call 1-888-266-4226.

For more information or to order direct, visit DarkHorse.com or call 1-800-862-0052 • Mon.–Fri. 9 a.m. to 5 p.m. Pacific Time.
Prices and availability subject to change without notice.